Meteorology

David Wright

**GEOGRAPHY
APPLIED**

General
Editor
JOHN
HANCOCK

BASIL BLACKWELL

Contents

Basil Blackwell
108 Cowley Rd
Oxford
OX4 1JF

First published 1983

ISBN 0 631 13256 2 (paperback edition)
     0 631 91340 8 (school edition)

Designed and typeset by FD Graphics Ltd., Fleet, Hampshire
Printed in Hong Kong

1 Introduction

It has been said that the most common topic of conversation in England is the weather. Perhaps that is because whoever we are talking to they are sure to have some interest in the subject. The weather affects almost everything we do and despite our increasing mastery over the environment we cannot yet control or even significantly change the weather. Many would claim we are unable to give a reliable prediction of what the weather will do, even for the next 24 hours, although the Meteorological Office reckons to be 93 per cent accurate over that period.

The real importance of the weather to the individual lies in its power to enhance or ruin those events in our lives that really matter. Most of us work indoors or in a protected environment and so the weather does not normally interfere a great deal with our working lives, but where leisure activities are concerned it is often fundamental to their success. It is depressing enough if the weather is bad during the week but at least it might be fine for the weekend. Good weather creates a feeling of well-being. We fervently hope that the sun will shine on our day by the sea, the church fête or the village cricket match. Even in winter good weather makes the air crisp and invigorating so that we are glad to be alive.

Bad weather can be annoying, frustrating, costly and sometimes extremely dangerous. It can cause wholesale cancellation of sporting events, ruin holidays or a day in the countryside, damage or destroy crops, cause the death of large numbers of livestock, disrupt communications and transport, and endanger life on land, at sea and in the air. Rarely does man feel so helpless as when confronted with the elements in all their fury.

2 Some meteorological disasters

The English weather is characterised by rapid change and we are quite used to its unreliability. In particular we cannot rely on it remaining dry for very long and this makes holidays in England a rather risky business.

It is not easy to find examples of long spells of fine weather but the summer of 1976 was a recent and outstanding example. By the end of August the landscape was mainly yellow and brown instead of the familiar green and it was more reminiscent of Spain than of England. Although it was certainly a summer to be enjoyed it had its problems, not least the supply of water for industrial and domestic consumption, and in the scarcity and therefore the high cost of animal feedstuffs.

Long spells of consistent weather are not only unusual, they are also impossible to forecast. Short term forecasts covering only a day or so are much more accurate and if heeded can save money and lives. On Monday, 13 August 1979 a small but deep depression was approaching the British Isles from the southwest. At the time the Fastnet Race for the Admirals Cup was in progress. During the night of the 13 and 14 August it crossed southern Ireland. The chart, figure 2.1, shows the situation as it existed at 06 hours on the Tuesday morning. A total of 306 yachts from 18 nations were taking part and most of them were scattered across the Celtic Sea between Cornwall and the Irish coast. During the night gusts of 129 km per hour were experienced and as a result 23 vessels were either sunk or abandoned, 106 retired and only 177 finished the course. Worst of all 17 lives were lost. With boats costing between £100,000 and £250,000 the final insurance bill was calculated to exceed five million pounds.

Fig 2.1   Depression centred over Ireland at 06 hours on Tuesday 14 August 1979

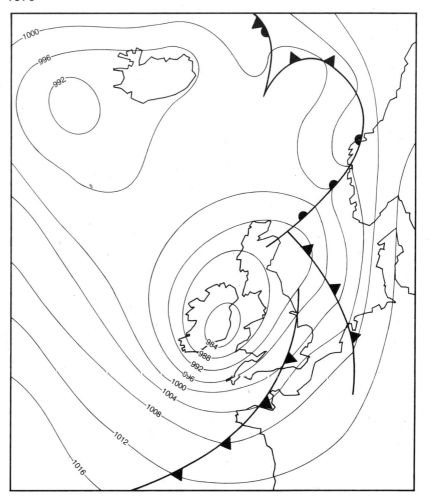

Such winds are unusual in Britain, although perhaps not so uncommon as we like to think. In areas where tropical hurricanes occur the bill for damage can be very much greater. Figure 2.2 shows the tracks of four hurricanes and their location on 11 September 1961. Hurricane Debbie had an extreme easterly track, affecting western Ireland where there were 17 deaths, and later Iceland. Hurricane Carla on the other hand moved much further west to affect the Gulf Coasts of Louisiana and eastern and central Texas (figure 2.3a).

The first warning came on 8 September when hurricane Carla, lying 720 km south of New Orleans, changed course towards the Gulf Coast. By 10 September 250,000 people had been evacuated from the most threatened areas. Carla struck later that night and the quiet eye at the centre of the storm passed over the coast of western Louisiana. The winds around the centre formed a belt over 160 km across with gusts of up to 278 km per hour. The tides produced by these winds were 3.6 m above normal and a large area was devastated. In Kaplan, Louisiana, 50 people were killed or injured while Galveston further west was also severely affected. As if floods and high winds were not enough to contend with, additional danger came from rattlesnakes which climbed walls to escape the rising waters!

In all half a million people fled from the disaster area and the road to Dallas and Fort Worth was jammed with cars bumper to bumper. Many evacuees were reported to be 'confused and frightened'.

By 12 September hurricane Carla had reached Austin but the winds had already dropped to a mere 80 km per hour. Tornadoes travelling in the wake of hurricane Carla continued to cause damage along the coast and one hit Galveston demolishing 100 wooden houses, killing 6 and injuring 60. An eye-witness wrote, 'Thousands of houses have been reduced to matchwood; many boats, including luxury yachts, have been driven ashore or sunk; factories and sheds have been levelled; thousands of cars have been wrecked, and the destruction of crops is widespread.' The final death toll of hurricane Carla was 21 but many hundreds of people were injured.

The final bill for insurance was between $85 million and $100 million, some of which was carried by British companies. In 1960 hurricane Donna caused $150 million worth of damage

but this was because it hit a more heavily populated area and not because of its greater size or intensity (figure 2.3b).

Strong winds can cause considerable problems on land as well as at sea. In January 1979 a depression centred over the Bay of Biscay brought snow and strong easterly winds to the west of England. Figure 10.3 on page 56 shows the situation at midnight on Friday, 5 January. Although snowfalls were not generally greater than 10-15 cm, there was much drifting in the strong to gale force easterly winds. By the time the storm had passed, the deep lanes of Somerset and Dorset had been filled in, especially where they ran north to south across the path of the wind, and behind every hedge and wall there were dune-like ridges of snow. Hundreds of vehicles were trapped and many more were completely buried in drifts up to 4.5 m deep (figure 2.3c).

Of all meteorological disasters, floods are probably the most costly. In December 1981 rain and melting snow, which had swollen West Country rivers, coincided with a tidal surge in the Bristol Channel backed by high winds. The sea walls which protect the low-lying Somerset Levels were breached in 30 places between Hinckley Point and Severn Beach north of Bristol, and hundreds of homes in Burnham-on-Sea, Minehead, Weston-super-Mare and Clevedon were flooded. The Wessex Water Authority worked hard to strengthen the defences with large quantities of stone brought from Mendip quarries and 2000 tons of concrete, but they could not withstand a high tide of 6.4 m in Bridgwater Bay (a detailed study of the Wessex Water Authority appears in *Hydrology* in this series).

A typical experience was that of Mr Hewlett, a farmer in the village of Wick St Lawrence. He was busy milking at the time when someone said the tide was coming up the lane. He ran out to see what was happening and found the water waist deep and full of sewage, moving slowly towards the farm. Although they worked hard to try to save the capons and Christmas turkeys being reared on the farm, more than a thousand birds were drowned causing a £5000 uninsured loss.

In all, more than 1000 houses were flooded and power cuts affected 30,000 homes in the region. Even then the disaster was small compared with the very similar events of February 1953 in Holland. Here there were 67 major

breaches in the sea dykes, some over 275 m across. The area flooded amounted to 152,000 hectares and much land was ruined by the salt. A total of 25,000 head of cattle were lost in this prosperous dairying region and worse still 1,800 people lost their lives. In all 47,000 houses were destroyed or damaged, and the final cost was reckoned to be around a hundred million pounds.

These are only a few examples of the numerous meteorological disasters which occur every year and in all parts of the world. It is when we realise the enormous cost in lives and property caused by these events that the true value of accurate weather forecasting becomes apparent. However good our understanding of the weather becomes it is unlikely that we will be able to prevent these disasters occurring, but we can minimise the cost given sufficient warning.

The study of weather has always been a very difficult one for man to undertake. Although the effects lie all around us the causes are high in the atmosphere or deep in the oceans and so rather inaccessible. Indeed processes in the air could only be observed from the ground, until balloons and later aircraft and rockets became available. The scale of meteorological phenomena is another problem, which was for a very long time aggravated by the scarcity of weather stations that could provide accurate data, and this state of affairs still applies to some extent in the southern hemisphere.

A third difficulty lies in the complexity of atmospheric processes, for weather is not just the result of a simple chain of cause and effect, but is the spatial expression of a web of inter-related phenomena. In its turn this poses severe problems to anyone who wishes to provide some account of the subject. In this book we have chosen to begin with the atmosphere, which is the environment within which the weather occurs. We then consider the sun, which is of course the energy source which drives the earth's weather machine, and the way in which the earth and its atmosphere are heated.

This could lead naturally to the way in which the atmosphere circulates as a result of the radiant heat received from the sun, followed by a consideration of the weather systems that grow and decay as they travel across the surface of the earth. However, neither the circulation of the atmosphere nor the

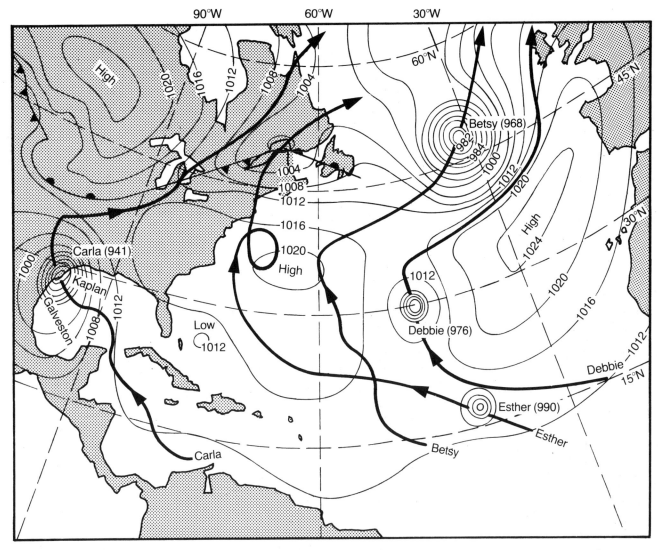

Fig 2.2   *The tracks of four hurricanes and their positions on 11 September 1961*

major weather systems can be fully understood without some appreciation of the vital role of water vapour in the atmosphere. We have therefore chosen to deal with water in the atmosphere first, and this is followed by atmospheric circulation and the nature of weather systems. Inevitably ideas are introduced which must be referred to again or even expanded at a later stage and it is important to realise that the book cannot be read simply from cover to cover. We therefore recommend a full use of the index provided. The book concludes with a consideration of local climate and the way in which weather is recorded and portrayed on weather maps.

EXERCISES

2.1 Examine your local newspaper or one of the national dailies over a period, and keep a record of the ways in which weather affects life in Britain.

2.2 Make a list of as many ways as you can in which you personally might benefit from good weather forecasts. Could you make better use of them than you have in the past?

2.3 Choose a sport (e.g., caving, sailing, mountain climbing, hang gliding) and find out what risks are involved due to adverse weather. What do you feel about people who participate in such sports and who therefore sometimes jeopardise the lives of others when they get into difficulties? Write an account of what you feel are the main arguments.

Fig 2.3a   Hurricane Carla destroys a yacht club in Texas, 11 September 1961

Fig 2.3b   A yacht caught in hurricane Donna in Boston, September 1960

Fig 2.3c   Heavy snow in Clyst Honiton, Devon, January 1979

Fig 2.3d   Serious flooding in York, January 1982

3 The atmosphere

Anyone who has flown in a modern jet aircraft at a height of 10 to 15 km above the surface of the earth will have been impressed by the view from the cabin window. We might describe the atmosphere as a deep ocean of air but reference to figure 3.1 shows that compared to the size of the solid earth the atmosphere is a very thin layer of gas indeed.

Any gas is highly compressible and the weight of the atmosphere causes the lower layers to be very much more dense than those above. A person standing on the summit of a mountain 5,500 m high would have exactly half of the mass of the atmosphere below them. As atmospheric pressure at any level depends on the weight of air above, pressure decreases logarithmically with height, and the air soon becomes very thin. Ninety-nine per cent of the atmosphere is contained in the first 32 km and above this it becomes progressively more tenuous so that an arbitrary outer limit only is drawn at a height of 1000 km.

Air pressure

An early measurement of the pressure of the atmosphere at sea level was made by the Italian scientist Torricelli who showed that it would support a column of mercury 760 mm high.

Pressure can be defined as force per unit area and today meteorologists use units called millibars (abbreviated as mb), one millibar being equal to 100 Newtons per square metre. (A Newton is a force which will accelerate a mass of 1 kg by 1m/sec².) Normal air pressure at mean sea level is 1,013 mb though it can vary from below 900 mb in a deep tropical depression to above 1,070 mb in an intense continental anticyclone.

As pressure is so closely related to height, meteorologists often work with constant pressure levels rather than constant heights. Thus sea level can be referred to as the 1000 mb surface while the average height of the 500 mb surface is 5,500 metres. In this way isobars or lines of equal pressure can be viewed rather like contours.

The composition of the atmosphere

The atmosphere is a mixture of gases, some of which are variable in their proportions. Of the fixed gases nitrogen contributes about 78 per cent of the atmosphere by volume and oxygen 21

per cent by volume, as measured for dry air. The final 1 per cent is made up of trace gases listed in figure 3.3. Water vapour is the most variable reaching as much as 4 per cent by volume in some localities and is usually concentrated in the first 10 – 15 km above the earth's surface. Ozone is produced from oxygen by ultra-violet radiation from the sun, and is found in the zone 30 – 80 km above the earth. Without its presence ultra-violet radiation would penetrate to the surface of the earth making life on the land impossible.

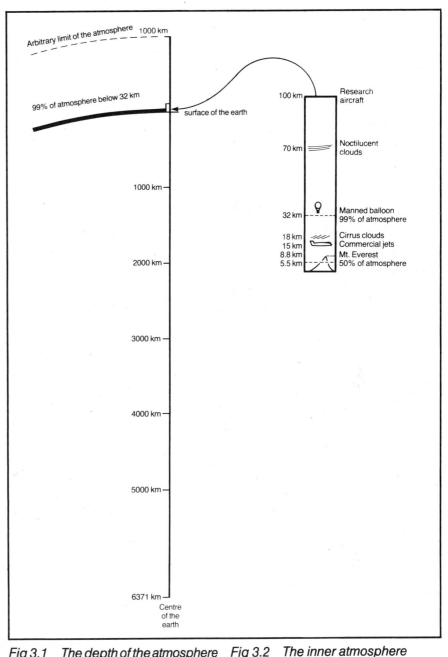

Fig 3.1   The depth of the atmosphere   Fig 3.2   The inner atmosphere

Fig 3.3   Approximate proportions of atmospheric gases by volume

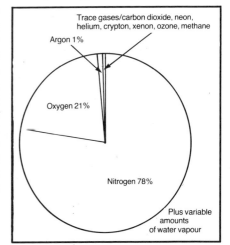

4 Heating the atmosphere

The sun's radiation

Although there is a flow of heat from the earth's interior due to the radioactive decay of atoms of such elements as uranium, it is small compared with that from the sun. When the sun is overhead, 25,000 (2.5×10^4) times as much energy falls on the earth's surface as flows from its interior.

The sun radiates energy into space in all directions equally. As the earth's average distance from the sun is 150 million (1.5×10^8) km, it intercepts only a very small part of the sun's total energy output. It is warmed in much the same way as a fly circling a bonfire at a distance of 30 m, and actually receives about one part in two thousand million (5×10^{-10}) of the total energy radiated. Despite this the radiant

Fig 4.1 A ladder of energy: examples of energy transfer are arranged in ascending order

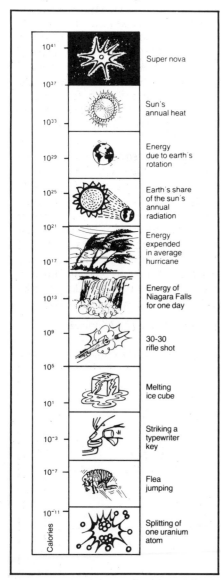

energy from the sun arriving at the earth, known as the solar constant, is 2 calories per sq cm per minute or 8.36 joules per sq cm per minute. This is equivalent to the energy that would be produced by 180 million large power stations or one hundred times greater than the total energy used on earth by man in a year.

We can use these figures to calculate the sun's total energy output. If we imagine the sun enclosed in a sphere whose radius is the distance from the earth to the sun, then 2 calories per minute (8.36 joules per minute) must fall on every square centimetre of the inner surface of that sphere. As the surface area of a sphere is $4 \pi R^2$ and R in this case is 1.5×10^{13} centimetres, the result is $4 \times 3.14 \times (1.5 \times 10^{13})^2$ which gives an area of 2.8×10^{27} sq cm. If each square centimetre receives 8.36 joules per minute then the total energy radiated is $8.36 \times 2.8 \times 10^{27}$ joules per minute. This is the same as saying that the sun radiates 4×10^{20} megawatts. If we assume that a very large power station produces 1000 megawatts then the sun is equivalent to 4×10^{17} power stations! (Examples of a range of energy transfers are shown in figure 4.1.)

We know from fossil evidence that the sun has been producing energy at this enormous rate for at least the last 3000 million years. Analysis of sunlight shows that the sun's surface layers consist of 70 per cent hydrogen and 25 per cent helium, and one way in which these vast amounts of energy could be produced is by the nuclear fusion process in which hydrogen is converted to helium. This yields 1.5×10^{11} calories for every gram of hydrogen converted to helium, which is more than enough to account for the sun's energy output over the last 3000 million years. It is believed that at this rate the sun has enough hydrogen left to go on doing this for another 60,000 million years, although some scientists think that structural changes in the sun may reduce its energy output in 5000 to 10,000 million years from now.

In a hot body like the sun there are many small charged particles such as electrons moving at high speeds and colliding with each other. These collisions produce waves called electromagnetic radiation. High speed collisions produce short waves and lower speed collisions long waves.

All of these electromagnetic waves travel at the same speed of 3×10^{10} cm or 300,000 km per second through

space. If we analyse the sun's radiant energy we find it consists of a whole family of electromagnetic radiations including x-rays, visible light, radiated heat and radio waves. As figure 4.2 shows, about half of this radiation is in the form of visible light and most of the rest is ultra-violet or infra-red radiation. It is surely not coincidence, but the result of evolution, that the eyes of men and animals are tuned in to radiation with wavelengths in the region of 5×10^{-5} cm as so much of the sun's energy is radiated in this form, most of which is able to penetrate the earth's atmosphere.

The temperature of a distant radiating body can be determined from its colour. At low temperatures the wavelength radiated most brightly is long and reddish in colour. At higher temperatures the wavelength radiated most brightly is shorter and the colour ranges from yellow to blue. The curve shown in figure 4.2 can be demonstrated to have come from an object with a surface temperature of about 6000°C.

The earth's heat balance

It has already been pointed out that life as we know it would not be possible on the earth if the atmosphere did not shield us from dangerous ultra-violet radiation. Even so, careless exposure to the sun can still cause serious burns. However, life on earth also depends heavily on the fact that temperatures at the earth's surface are such as to allow water to exist in all three states: liquid, vapour and ice. If this were not so the water cycle could not operate and the continents would be barren.

Throughout much of geological time the earth appears to have been warmer than it is now. During the past 60 million years the average surface temperature has fallen from a warm 22°C to as low as 2°C at the time of the furthest extent of the polar ice sheets. Records show, however, that the earth's surface temperature has varied little from its present average of 15°C over the past few centuries. This suggests that the earth is now emitting the same amount of energy into space as it receives from the sun. If it were not so then the energy would accumulate, or dissipate into space, and the surface temperature would change accordingly. If objects are not in radiative balance with their surroundings then temperature changes occur to re-establish the equilibrium. In the case of the human

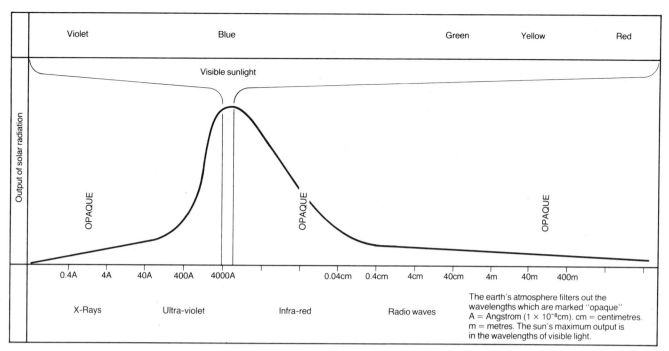

Fig 4.2   The energy spectrum of the sun

body a higher but constant temperature is maintained by the intake of food. The earth also has a constant energy source and so has a constant temperature and this is largely determined by the distance of the earth from the sun. Figure 4.3 shows the temperatures of the planets assuming them to be in radiative balance with their surroundings.

It is true that the earth is slightly nearer the sun in early January than it is in early July but this has only a very small effect. The sun's energy output also varies by one or two per cent but this too is not significant unless it can be shown to act as a trigger mechanism, and so the earth is very nearly in radiative balance with its surroundings and its average temperature remains the same from year to year.

The heat budget

Incoming solar radiation, or insolation, is short wave radiation and for con-venience we can imagine the total insolation reaching the earth as 100 units. The atmosphere is fairly transparent to short wave radiation and as figure 4.4 shows 47 of these units are able to reach the earth's surface. A further 17 units are absorbed by the atmosphere, 2 of these by the ozone in the stratosphere and 15 by ozone, water vapour and clouds in the troposphere. Dust and water droplets in the lower atmosphere promote scattering at the blue end of the spectrum and this is what causes the colour of our clear skies. This scattering accounts for 22 units of insolation, 6 of which are lost to space and 16 of which penetrate to the earth's surface.

Further losses result from the reflection of insolation by the upper surfaces of clouds and from the surface of the earth. The percentage of radiation reflected is called the albedo. Pictures of the earth from space show that about half of the surface has cloud cover at any given time and this causes 23 units to be reflected into space. The reflection of insolation by the solid earth is more complicated. It depends on the angle of incidence of the incoming radiation and therefore on the latitude and on the nature of the surface. Fresh snow may reflect as much as 90 per cent, farmland around 20 per cent and forest about 10 per cent. Overall the albedo of the earth's surface accounts for about 7 units giving a total figure for the planetary albedo of 36 units.

The incoming radiation which successfully penetrates the atmosphere serves to heat the earth. The outgoing terrestrial radiation is called black-body radiation and is equivalent to 98 units of long wave radiation in the infra-red part of the spectrum. This cannot pass through the atmosphere so easily and figure 4.4 shows that 91 units are absorbed, chiefly by carbon dioxide, water vapour and clouds. Only 7 units are directly radiated back into space.

Fig 4.3   If the planets absorbed and emitted all the energy reaching them from the sun, they would have the temperatures shown by the curve

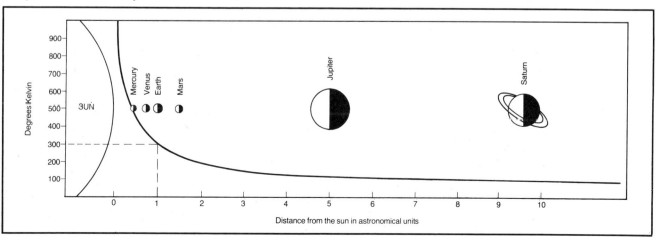

7

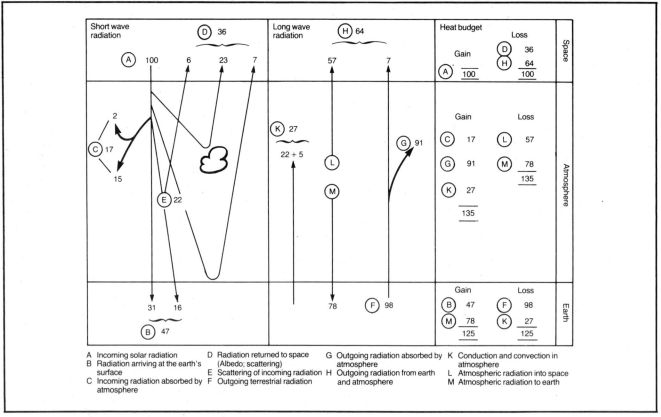

Fig 4.4   The earth's heat budget

As the atmosphere is heated by incoming and outgoing radiation as well as by conduction and convection, it too contributes to the heat budget. Water vapour is produced by evaporation at the surface of the earth and carried upwards by convection. The water vapour soon condenses into water droplets releasing latent heat into the atmosphere. Turbulence also carries warm air up into the earth's atmosphere. Convection accounts for 22 units while conduction accounts for only 5 units. As a result the atmosphere is able to radiate 78 units back to the earth's surface and 57 units out into space.

The vertical transfer of heat in the atmosphere as summarised in figure 4.4 also demonstrates that the earth, the atmosphere and the whole planetary system are in radiative balance with their surroundings. More important still it shows that whilst the atmosphere lets in short wave radiation from the sun fairly easily it is not so transparent to outgoing long wave radiation from the earth. The atmosphere thus acts as a kind of blanket creating what is known as the greenhouse effect and this phenomenon is very significant in determining the average surface temperature of the earth.

The thermal stratification of the atmosphere

It has long been known that temperature tends to decrease with altitude from such evidence as that of snow-capped mountains. This makes sense when we remember that the atmosphere allows the short wave solar radiation in, but is less transparent to outgoing long wave terrestrial radiation. This means that short wave radiation tends to heat the surface of the earth rather than the atmosphere so that the atmosphere is heated mainly from below. This is the reason why temperatures in the troposphere fall at an average of 6.5°C per km.

From the evidence of instruments carried by balloons, rockets and satellites we know that there are two further zones of heating in the upper atmosphere. These are shown in figure 4.5. The first occurs at a height of 16 km above the equator and 8 km above the poles, and continues to an altitude of 50 km. To begin with the temperature remains steady in a zone called the tropopause. This steady temperature prevents rising air from continuing upwards and so confines the phenomenon we refer to as weather to the troposphere. Further away from the earth's surface in the stratosphere, temperatures rise due to the absorption of incoming ultra-violet radiation by

Fig 4.5   The thermal stratification of the atmosphere

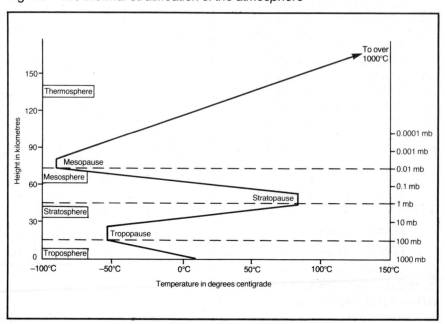

the ozone. As this process begins at the outer edge of the stratosphere this part is most exposed to the radiation and it is here that the highest temperatures are reached.

Above 50 km the rise in temperature ceases, remains steady at the stratopause, and then resumes its downward trend in the mesosphere. This continues to a height of 80 km where once more the temperature steadies at the mesopause and then rises in the thermosphere. This time the rise in temperature is due to absorption of incoming ultra-violet radiation by atomic oxygen. Above 100 km the atmosphere is increasingly affected by solar X-rays and ultra-violet radiation, which separate negatively charged electrons from oxygen atoms and nitrogen molecules, causing a zone of ionization. The Aurora Borealis and the Aurora Australis result from the penetration of the upper atmosphere by ionized particles down to a height of 80 km above the earth's surface.

EXERCISES

4.1 Heat is transferred by the processes of conduction, convection and radiation. Which of these processes is most effective in each of the following examples:
(a) The cooling of a cup of tea
(b) Heating a pan of water on the cooker
(c) Warming your bed with an electric blanket
(d) Getting a suntan?
4.2 Why do substances containing radio-active elements tend to become warmer than their environment?
4.3 Since the earth radiates thermal energy, why is it not listed as a contributor to the sun's heat?
4.4 Trace the heat energy of your body back to the sun as source.
4.5 Calculate the amount of solar energy radiated to Mars given that

$$\frac{\text{Sun} - \text{Mars distance}}{\text{Sun} - \text{Earth distance}} = 1.5$$

and

$$\frac{\text{Radius of Mars}}{\text{Radius of Earth}} = 0.54$$

Compare this result with the corresponding figure for the energy radiated to the earth.

Variability in insolation

So far our discussion has only been concerned with the earth's average surface temperature, but reference to figure 4.6 shows that there are great variations, ranging from a July average of $-60°C$ over the south pole to an average $30°C$ over the hot deserts of the northern hemisphere in the same month. The Greeks were well aware of the decrease in temperature with latitude and on that basis divided the world into torrid, temperate and frigid zones.

This results largely from the decrease in the angle of incidence of the sun's rays with increasing latitude with the result that insolation is spread over an ever increasing area, so reducing its effectiveness. At the same time the journey through the atmosphere is greater, resulting in more absorption and scattering of sunlight in high latitudes, than in the tropics (see figure 4.7). A low angle of incidence increases the earth's albedo, especially over the oceans, while the large expanses of ice and snow around the poles add to the

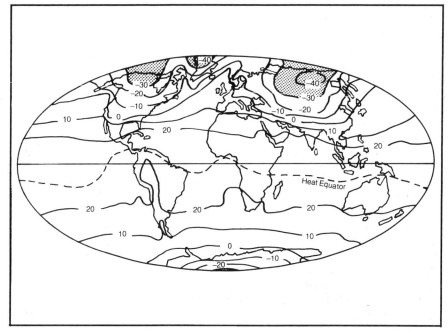

Fig 4.6a   Surface temperatures in January

Fig 4.6b   Surface temperatures in July

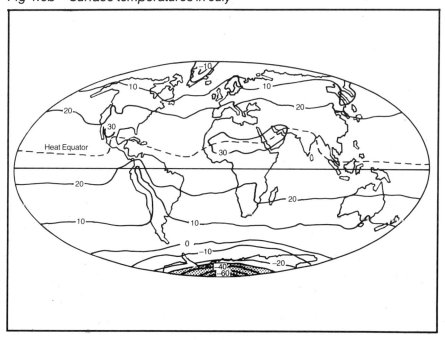

amount of sunlight reflected from the surface of the earth.

There is also a seasonal effect resulting from the way in which the earth moves in space. In addition to its revolution about the sun, the earth rotates about an imaginary axis inclined at an angle of 66½° to the elliptic, or the plane of its orbit. As figure 4.8 shows, the direction of tilt of the axis remains constant and so changes with respect to the sun through the year. In June the northern hemisphere is tilted directly towards the sun and this increases the length of the day and the angle of incidence of the sun's rays giving summer. Winter occurs in the southern hemisphere because here the axis is tilted away from the sun giving the opposite effect. In December the situation is reversed in each hemisphere and the southern hemisphere has summer and the northern hemisphere winter. These positions are known as the solstices while the midway positions in March and September are the equinoxes.

EXERCISES

4.6 Explain what is special about the polar circles, the tropics and the equator in terms of the length of the day through the year and the occurrence of the overhead sun. Reference to figure 4.8 should provide the answers.

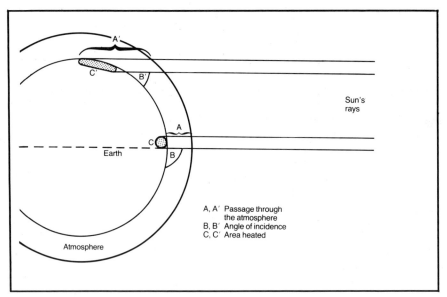

Fig 4.7   The effectiveness of insolation

4.7 Draw a diagram based on the information in figure 4.8 to show the earth midway between December and March, paying special attention to the position of the line dividing day from night.

4.8 At 15° north latitude there are two periods during the year when temperature maxima occur. Locations at latitudes greater than 23½° north experience only one such period. Explain.

4.9 Attempt to describe the conditions on the earth if it behaved like the planet Uranus, so that its axis of rotation always pointed the same way but lay in the plane of its orbit. (It may help to redraw figure 4.8 making the appropriate alterations.)

Another important cause of temperature differences at the earth's surface is the disposition of land and sea. Continents and oceans respond very differently to incoming solar radiation. In low latitudes where the sun is at an angle of 60° or more, the albedo is only 2 or 3 per cent over the oceans, but in high latitudes it can be 80 or 90 per cent. The thermal equivalent (i.e., the number of joules required to raise the temperature of 1 gm of a substance by 1°C) of water is far greater than that of soil and rocks. Water therefore takes more energy to heat it, and the process takes longer. However, once water is warm it contains a great deal of heat energy and so it takes longer to cool down. The result is that temperature variations are much smaller over the

Fig 4.8   The earth's journey around the sun

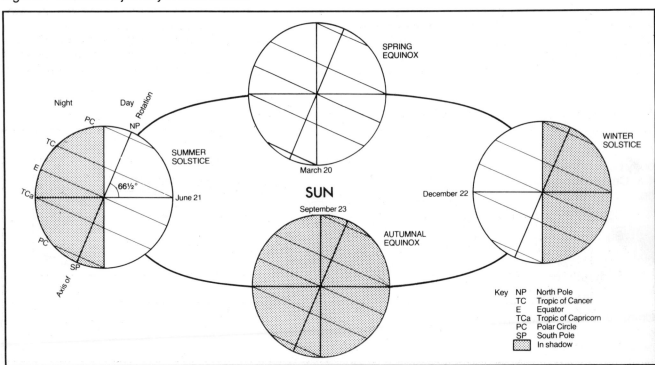

oceans than over the land. The water of the oceans is also fairly transparent allowing sunlight to penetrate to a considerable depth and in tropical waters 10 per cent of the radiation may reach 10 m below the surface. The role of the oceans as reservoirs of heat is a fundamental one, and coastal areas have more equable climates than inland areas. In the same way the larger proportion of ocean in the southern hemisphere means that southern summers are cooler than northern ones while southern winters are milder.

Heat transfer in the atmosphere

Figure 4.9 shows the variation in the earth's heat budget with latitude. One curve shows the average amount of energy absorbed by the earth and atmosphere at each latitude during the year. The other shows the amount of energy emitted at each latitude during the year and it is clear that regions at low latitudes absorb more energy than they emit and those at higher latitudes emit more energy than they absorb. For this state of imbalance to be maintained there must be some compensating transfer of heat from low latitudes to high latitudes, otherwise temperatures would rise in the tropics and fall around the poles.

Up to 80 per cent of this energy transfer is achieved by the circulation of the atmosphere. In detail this circulation is very complicated but put very simply large-scale convection currents carry warm air polewards and cold air towards the equator. At the same time

vast quantities of water vapour produced by evaporation from the surface of the oceans in the tropics are carried polewards, and when the vapour condenses in colder regions it releases latent heat. (Details of the circulation of the atmosphere are to be found in chapter 6.)

Ocean currents also make an important contribution to the transfer of heat energy between the tropics and the polar regions. Some movement of water is due to density differences, especially in the deeper parts of the ocean basins. An increase in density may be the result of evaporation and subsequent increase in salinity in tropical regions or due to surface cooling and the addition of glacial melt water near the poles. The Gulf of Mexico is an example of a region of high salinity, while the east coast of Greenland and the Weddell Sea of Antarctica are areas where cold dense water accumulates. Cold dense water naturally has a tendency to sink and then moves slowly across the ocean floors where it may stay for periods of 500 to 1000 years. Accumulation of such cold water, perhaps resulting from the geologically recent location of the continents, may have played an important part in the cause of the ice age.

The slow vertical circulation of water caused by density differences plays a very minor role in heat transfer but it is worth noting that cold water tends to be confined in the Arctic Ocean by the surrounding land masses and the ridges across the North Atlantic and the Bering Sea, while that around the Antarctic continent is much more widespread in its distribution.

Much more important in heat transfer are the surface currents of water that are driven by the prevailing wind

systems. Such movement of water is well illustrated by the situation in the North Atlantic shown in figure 4.10. Surface water near the equator is urged westward by the trade winds and enters the Gulf of Mexico. The accumulated water piles up against the American continent and because of its relatively high temperature it cannot escape by sinking and so overflows through the Florida Strait as a strong stream running at an average of 3 knots. As far as Cape Kennedy it flows parallel with the coast of the United States, but here it comes under the influence of the westerly winds which drive it northwestwards towards Europe.

During its passage across the Atlantic the Gulf Stream broadens and becomes a surface drift of water rather than a current and is therefore better known as the North Atlantic Drift. The actual surface temperature of the water is only a few degrees warmer than the average for its latitude, but this is sufficient to bring a significant warming influence to the whole of Northwest Europe. It has been shown that if 1,200 sq km of ocean, 180 m deep, were to cool by half a centigrade degree, enough heat would be released to raise the temperature of the atmosphere by five centigrade degrees over the whole of Europe. The result of all this is an ice-free coast well beyond Norway's North Cape and including the Russian port of Murmansk. Meanwhile across the Atlantic the coasts of Labrador, Newfoundland and Nova Scotia are icebound in winter, and ice floats about in New York harbour on the same latitude as Rome!

In general the circulation of ocean water is influenced by the rotation of the earth on its axis, the configuration

Fig 4.9 Heat budget for the earth with latitude

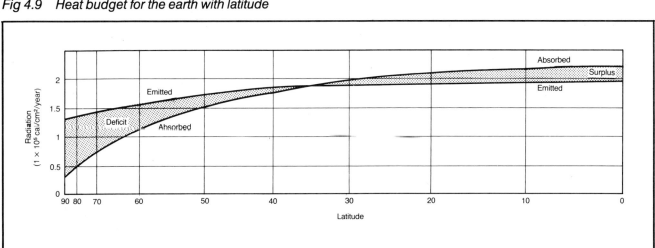

of ocean basins and continents and the pattern of the earth's atmospheric circulation. It is clockwise in the northern hemisphere and anti-clockwise in the southern hemisphere (see figure 4.11). The net effect of this is to carry cold water towards the equator along the eastern margins of ocean basins and warm water towards the poles along the western margins, thus contributing to the heat exchange between the tropics and the polar regions.

EXERCISES

4.10 What is probably the chief source of the sun's energy?

4.11 If you continue heating a red hot poker or branding iron to raise its temperature, will it become blue hot? Explain.

4.12 If the earth were twice its present distance from the sun what would be its approximate temperature?

4.13 How do water vapour and carbon dioxide keep the earth's surface warmer?

4.14 What effect do you think a great increase in water vapour in the earth's atmosphere would have on the average surface temperature?

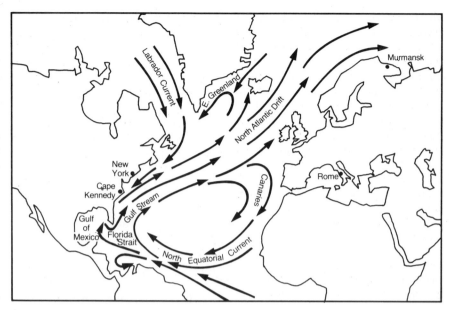

Fig 4.10   Ocean currents in the North Atlantic

4.15 What factors cause the earth's seasons?

4.16 What causes the lag of the seasons?

4.17 Records show that the entire earth's average temperature is higher during the northern hemisphere summer when the earth is farthest from the sun than it is during the northern hemisphere winter when the earth is closest to the sun. Knowing that the major part of the earth's land masses is in the northern hemisphere, can you suggest why the earth's average temperature is higher when it is farthest from the sun?

Fig 4.11   A simplified map of the world's ocean currents

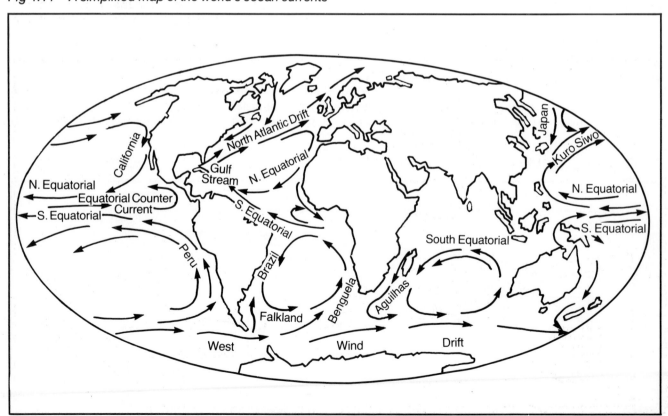

5 Water in the atmosphere

All life on the earth depends on the presence of water. Water is a unique substance and as we have already seen one of its most valuable properties is that it exists naturally in the atmosphere in all three states: solid as in snowflakes and hailstones; liquid as in fog, cloud and raindrops; gaseous as in water vapour. Other similar substances with low molecular weights have much lower freezing and boiling points than 0°C and 100°C and so vaporise at normal atmospheric temperatures. If water behaved like this there would be no liquid water and no life on earth at all as we know it.

The exchange of water molecules between the atmosphere on the one hand, and the oceans and continents on the other, depends to a very large extent on temperature changes and the way these affect the ability of the atmosphere to hold water vapour. Generally speaking high temperatures encourage evaporation and an increase in the humidity or water content of the atmosphere, while low temperatures promote condensation and precipitation. At the same time the way in which these processes operate depends very greatly on the unique character of the water molecule. A knowledge of the structure of water molecules and the way they are bonded together in ice and water is fundamental to the appreciation of the concepts of evaporation, condensation and humidity.

The hydrological cycle

The availability of water is no problem for life in the oceans but life on land can only exist because water readily undergoes changes of state when heated or cooled, through the processes of evaporation, condensation and precipitation. The result is the circulation of water between the ocean, the atmosphere and the land in the hydrological cycle, details of which are shown in figure 5.1. A more detailed discussion of the hydrological cycle appears in *Hydrology* in this series.

The diagram shows the circulation of water through the three phases of the cycle. The oceans (A) may be thought of as the main reservoir of water. Movements of water in the oceans include vertical ones resulting from differences in density and salinity, and surface drift of water due to the prevailing winds in the main ocean currents.

Phase B shows the atmospheric stage of the cycle. This can be subdivided into exchanges between the atmosphere and the ocean (B_1), where on balance there is a gain in moisture content by the atmosphere, and into exchanges between the atmosphere and the land (B_2) where on balance there is a loss in moisture content by the atmosphere. As in the oceans, however, moisture is again redistributed within the atmosphere, this time by vertical movements of the air as for example in thermals and by horizontal movements due to winds.

Phase C of the cycle is often referred to as the drainage basin cycle. Here water that has fallen as precipitation follows a number of possible pathways on its way back to the sea. Rainfall normally infiltrates into the soil and moves downhill through the underlying rock as groundwater flow or through the soil as through flow. If rainfall is so heavy that it exceeds the infiltration rate of the soil then it becomes run off in the form of overland flow. Alternatively if the soil is already saturated with water, infiltration will be at a minimum and run off will again occur, this time as saturated overland flow. Most of this water will find its way into rivers and streams: groundwater through springs, soilwater through seepage, and runoff directly into the stream channel from both banks. Some precipitation, however, will be intercepted by leaves and evaporated back into the atmosphere along with a proportion of the soil water, while plants will take up soilwater through their roots and return it to the atmosphere by transpiration. This combined loss of water back to the atmosphere is referred to as evapotranspiration.

At any time more than 97 per cent of the water on the earth is contained in the oceans and more than 2 per cent in lakes and rivers and in the soil and rock of the continents as groundwater. This leaves only a fraction of 1 per cent in the atmosphere and yet its presence is fundamental to the weather of our

Fig 5.1 The hydrological cycle

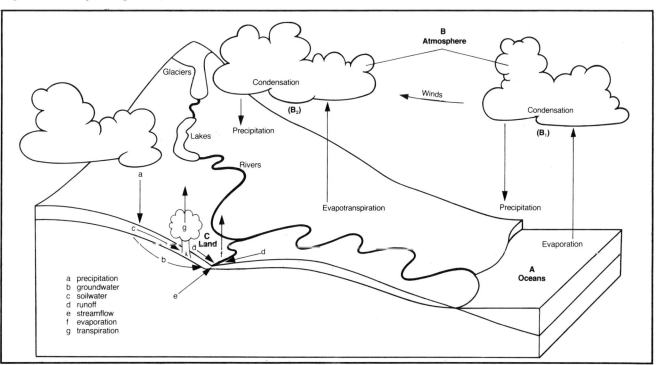

a precipitation
b groundwater
c soilwater
d runoff
e streamflow
f evaporation
g transpiration

planet. As we have already seen water vapour is responsible for intercepting radiation from the sun and for large-scale heat exchanges through the processes of evaporation and condensation. On a more local scale it is an active ingredient in depressions and thunderstorms; all forms of precipitation of water vapour make a crucial contribution to weather.

EXERCISES

5.1 Use the following figures to produce a statistical diagram.

The distribution of the earth's water (figures in millions of cubic kilometres)

Oceans	1,320
Glaciers and ice caps	30
Underground	9
Lakes and inland seas	0.23
Rivers and streams	0.001
Atmosphere	0.013

5.2 What does man need water for? Which water on the graph is useful and available to man and what percentage of the total is it?
5.3 How is fresh water produced by the sun? Why can't we de-salinate water cheaply, the same way? Why would a cheap method of de-salination be extremely useful to man? What source of fresh water is at present largely untapped by man?
5.4 Describe some of the ways in which water can be diverted from the basin water cycle.

Evapotranspiration

For a long time discussions of weather and climate took very little account of moisture losses through evapotranspiration and concerned themselves only with total precipitation and its distribution through the year. However, the effectiveness of precipitation is important for natural vegetation and for the farmer, and to ignore it very much reduces the practical value of the study of meteorology.

Early attempts to describe climates used temperature and precipitation as the primary criteria. A fine example of this would be the classification of W. Köppen which he devised between 1900 and 1936 (see figure 5.2). Of course the temperature regime will have a profound effect on evapotranspiration and in 1931 the American meteorologist and climatologist C.W. Thornthwaite

produced an expression for 'precipitation efficiency' obtained by relating measurements of pan evaporation to temperature and precipitation. This expression produced a monthly ratio (see figure 5.2) while the sum of the twelve monthly ratios was used to produce a precipitation efficiency (P.E.) index.

Later in 1948 Thornthwaite developed his ideas further when he employed a new concept which he called potential evapotranspiration. This is a very complex function to calculate, but in simple terms it represents the moisture losses from the soil by evaporation and transpiration whether or not there is soil moisture to be lost. Perhaps the most useful results of Thornthwaite's work are the graphs of moisture balance which can be produced. These not only show which periods in the year have either a net moisture loss or a net moisture gain but also whether there is a soil moisture surplus or a soil moisture deficiency, or whether the soil moisture storage is being depleted or recharged. Graphs

showing these changes in the moisture balance for Seattle, Washington and Grand Junction, Colorado are shown in figure 5.3.

The water molecule

It is now necessary for us to look more closely at the process of evaporation. At any time there is about 1.7×10^{13} tonnes (1.7×10^{15} kg) of water vapour in the earth's atmosphere, enough to produce more than an inch of rain (25.5 mm) over the entire earth. Most of this water vapour is produced by evaporation over the oceanic areas between 40°N and 40°S where high temperatures throughout the year facilitate the process, but lesser amounts are produced at other latitudes and by evapotranspiration over the land. This water vapour is distributed throughout the atmosphere by winds so that even in the heart of the world's great deserts there is plenty of moisture in the air. The aridity there is simply due to the absence of any process which will cause condensation.

Fig 5.2   Classification of climate

Koppen's classification of climate

Af	Tropical rain forest.
Am	Tropical monsoon.
Aw	Tropical savanna.
Bsh	Tropical steppe.
Bsk	Mid-latitude steppe.
Bwh	Tropical desert.
Bwk	Mid-latitude desert.
Cfa	Humid sub-tropical.
Cfb	Marine. Warm summer.
Cfc	Marine. Cool summer.
Csa	Interior mediterranean.
Csb	Coastal mediterranean.
Cwa	Sub-tropical monsoon.
Cwb	Tropical upland.
Dfa	Humid continental. Hot summer.
Dfb	Humid continental. Warm summer.
Dfc	Sub-arctic. Short summer.
Dfd	Sub-arctic. Very cold winter.
Dwa	Humid continental. Hot summer.
Dwb	Humid continental. Warm summer.
Dwc	Sub-arctic. Cold winter.
Dwd	Sub-arctic. Extremely cold winter.
ET	Tundra.
EF	Ice cap.
H	Highland climates.

Code
Second letter

f	rain all months
F	ice cap
m	rain forest despite short dry season
s	summer dry season
S	steppe
T	tundra
w	winter dry season
W	desert

Third letter

a	hot summer
b	warm summer
c	cool short summer
d	very cold winter
h	dry, hot
k	dry, cold

Thornthwaite's classification

P.E. Index (I)

$$I = \text{sum of twelve monthly values of } 115 \frac{P}{T-10}$$

where P = mean monthly precipitation in inches
T = mean monthly temperature in °F

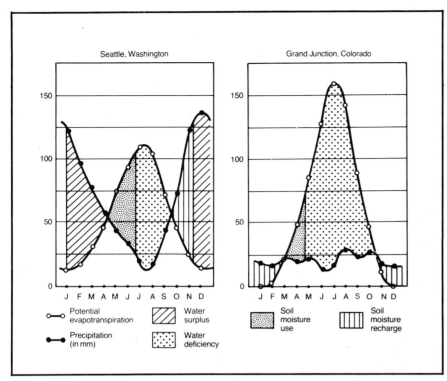

Fig 5.3   Graphs of potential evapotranspiration and precipitation for Seattle and Grand Junction

We shall be able to understand evaporation and condensation better if we know more about the nature of the water molecule. Each molecule is composed of two atoms of hydrogen and one atom of oxygen. The oxygen atom carries eight electrons, or more accurately electron clouds, around the nucleus. Two of these electrons form an inner shell and the remaining six an outer shell. In contrast each of the hydrogen atoms possesses a single electron.

As figure 5.4 shows, when atoms of hydrogen and oxygen are combined in the water molecule the electrons are arranged in pairs. Two of the pairs are composed of four of the electrons from the outer shell of the oxygen atom, while the other two pairs share one electron from the oxygen atom and one

electron from a hydrogen atom. This sharing of electrons makes a very strong bond called a hydrogen bond and also means there must always be two hydrogen atoms linked to each oxygen atom.

For simplicity figure 5.4 has been drawn with the hydrogen atoms on opposite sides of the oxygen atom but of course a water molecule has a three-dimensional arrangement. In reality the two hydrogen atoms are separated by an angular distance of 106° on one side of the oxygen while the two electron pairs are found on the other side as shown in figure 5.5. We can therefore visualise the water molecule as having four bulges located at the corners of a tetrahedron, each bulge corresponding with either a hydrogen atom or an electron pair.

The result of this arrangement is that

the negatively charged electrons are pulled away from the hydrogen nuclei by the nucleus of the oxygen atom, giving this end of the molecule a positive charge. At the other end the two electron pairs produce a negative charge resulting in a biased molecule which is referred to as a dipole.

The nature of ice
In ice crystals the water molecules are linked by all four corners to neighbouring molecules in a rigid tetrahedral arrangement. The result is a solid with a very open lattice containing large voids within it. If we consider each molecule to be essentially spherical it is possible to demonstrate that twelve similar molecules can be packed in contact around it (see figure 5.6). In the case of the ice crystal there are only four and this is what gives rise to the spaces in the lattice. It is these spaces which account for the expansion that occurs when water freezes and for the fact that, being lighter than water, ice floats.

Change of state
At 0°C ice begins to melt. What actually happens is that some of the hydrogen bonds are broken and the tetrahedral structure begins to decay. As the change progresses the spaces within the lattice begin to be occupied by single or linked molecules that have been freed from the lattice. As a result there is some contraction and an increase in density which continues until the temperature reaches 4°C when a more normal expansion and decrease in density ensues.

In the liquid state molecules or very small groups of molecules are free to move about relative to each other. The force of attraction between the molecules is, however, still quite strong resulting in considerable cohesion, and the distance between the molecules remains small. As the temperature continues to rise the molecules become more mobile until some molecules are able to overcome the forces binding them to the water surface and they break away, resulting in evaporation. Such free molecules remain relatively isolated and have the random motion that is typical of the gaseous state.

Energy changes
At the melting and evaporation stages energy is required to achieve the increased freedom of the molecules. In the case of water the energy required is extraordinarily high because not only

Fig 5.4   Hydrogen bonding in the water molecule

Fig 5.5   The tetrahedral arrangement of the water molecule

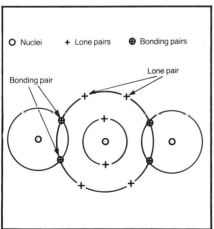

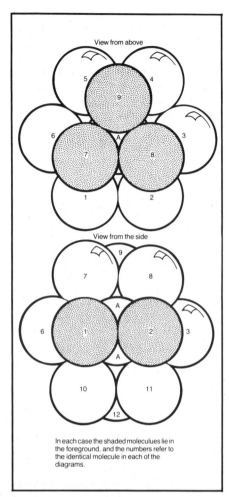

Fig 5.6 *Close packing of spherical molecules*

In each case the shaded moleculues lie in the foreground, and the numbers refer to the identical molecule in each of the diagrams.

must the mutual attraction of the molecules be overcome but the strong hydrogen bonds must also be broken. At the melting stage only some of these bonds are broken but it still requires 334 joules (80 cals) per gramme of ice melted to achieve the change. At the evaporation stage all the remaining bonds must be broken and so it requires 2,257 joules (540 cals) per gramme of water vaporised.

The energy used to melt ice or evaporate water is locked up as potential energy due to the increased separation of the molecules and in kinetic energy as a result of their increased motion. This energy will be released as latent heat whenever condensation or freezing occurs.

The large amount of energy involved is extremely important for meteorology. If the sun should for some reason increase its energy output much of the extra heat would result in increased evaporation in the tropics and melting ice in the polar regions. The temperature at the earth's surface would not change a great deal. Alternatively if the sun's energy output were to decrease the ice sheets would expand and there would be increased condensation of atmospheric vapour. Again the temperatures at the earth's surface would change less than might be expected. The role of the oceans as a storehouse of energy is a vital one for the world's climate.

Humidity

Water vapour like other gases is quite dry and perfectly invisible in the atmosphere. The white cloud that comes from a boiling kettle is not vapour or even steam but minute droplets of liquid water that have condensed in the cool air. In the same way mist, fog and clouds are not water vapour either, but are also made up of water droplets less than 0.05 mm (50 μm) in diameter, or in the case of clouds, water droplets or small crystals of ice.

Like all other substances water consists of molecules in constant motion. We have seen that as temperature rises this motion increases and some of the molecules are able to escape from the surface of the water. At the same time molecules of water in the air above are also in motion and some will collide with the water surface. So long as the number of molecules leaving the water surface exceeds the number returning then we can say that evaporation is taking place.

The number of molecules of water present per unit volume of air is known as humidity. As evaporation proceeds the population of water molecules in the air increases and so the number of molecules colliding with the water surface also increases. If the temperature now becomes steady and ceases to rise the rate at which molecules escape from the water will also become constant, and eventually the number of molecules leaving the water will be matched by those that return and a balance will have been achieved. At this point the air above the water is said to be *saturated*.

A further rise in temperature will cause the molecules in the water to move still faster and once more the number entering the atmosphere will exceed the number returning. Eventually a new balance will be achieved in which molecules will be exchanged between the water and the air at a faster rate and in which the population of molecules in the air will have been increased. Once again the air is saturated but clearly the number of molecules per unit volume of air has become greater. This explains a very important principle, namely that warm air can contain more water vapour than cold air.

To be able to visualise this a few quantities may be helpful. At a room temperature of 15°C, 12.7 grammes of water vapour will saturate a cubic metre of air. A room 5 m × 4 m × 2.5 m has a volume of 50 cu m and so could hold a maximum of 635 grammes of dry invisible vapour at 15°C. This means that if we could extract all the vapour from the atmosphere in such a room and turned it into water there would be 635 cc, or enough to fill two and a half average sized tumblers. Ordinarily the air is not saturated, but even for normal values the room would contain as much as 500 cc or the equivalent of two glasses of water. This is a surprising amount when you remember the water is there in vapour form, quite invisible and quite dry.

As all forms of precipitation depend on the amount of water vapour present in the atmosphere it is clearly important for us to be able to measure the humidity. This is not as simple as it may seem as the capacity of the air to hold water vapour depends on the temperature. For this reason we can either measure the water vapour content per unit volume of air which is known as the absolute humidity, or calculate how much of the air's capacity to hold water vapour has been taken up for a given temperature. This is known as the relative humidity and is expressed as a percentage of the maximum value for that temperature.

The most satisfactory way of defining humidity is in terms of vapour pressure. We have already seen that normal air pressure at sea level is 1,013 mb. Each of the gases that makes up the atmosphere contributes to this pressure. Thus at sea level, nitrogen has a partial pressure of 750 mb, oxygen 230 mb and water vapour from 5 mb to 30 mb. The pressure is due to the activity of the molecules of each gas and is proportional to the number of molecules present in the atmosphere.

The pressure due to the presence of water molecules in the atmosphere is called the vapour pressure and as evaporation takes place the vapour pressure increases. When this pressure just balances that within the liquid driving the molecules away from the water surface, evaporation appears to stop. The vapour pressure at which this occurs is the saturation vapour pressure and its value will increase as the temperature rises.

Using these ideas, absolute humidity becomes the partial pressure of the water vapour content or the actual vapour pressure, and relative humidity the ratio of the actual vapour pressure to the saturation vapour pressure expressed as a percentage, i.e.:

$$\frac{\text{actual vapour pressure}}{\text{saturation vapour pressure}} \times 100$$

For example, if the actual vapour pressure is 10 mb and the saturation vapour pressure is 25 mb then the relative humidity is $\frac{10}{25} \times 100$ or 40 per cent.

The physiological effects of humidity
The humidity of the air has important physiological effects and values of relative humidity that are comfortable for human beings are usually between 50 per cent and 75 per cent. If we are surrounded by air with a high relative humidity we say the atmosphere is stuffy and we begin to feel sleepy. This is because when we breathe we fill the innumerable tubes in our lungs with air. The oxygen in the air passes through the 'skin' of these tubes into the tiny blood vessels that surround them and this serves to oxygenate the blood. At the same time carbon dioxide passes in the reverse direction and we breathe out this unwanted gas. The air tubes in the lungs are lined with moisture in just the same way as the inside of the mouth. This is mostly water and is maintained with fresh supplies from the blood which balance the evaporation losses which occur when we breathe. If the air we breathe is heavily charged with moisture the evaporation takes place more slowly than usual. As the blood continues to make fresh supplies of water available at a more or less constant rate the lungs become somewhat choked with water and the lining of the air tubes thickens. This extra thickness makes the exchange of oxygen and carbon dioxide more difficult and less efficient and the blood is neither fully energised nor purified and we feel less alert in consequence.

Activity is also more difficult in a humid environment. When we exert ourselves the body generates additional heat which we lose by perspiring through the pores in our skin. This works well so long as the moisture is lost into the air by evaporation. If, however, the air is already saturated, the moisture will not be removed and

our clothing will soon become very damp with excess perspiration. Worse still the pores become clogged with moisture and the body is unable to get rid of surplus heat in an efficient way and so we begin to feel very uncomfortable, putting strain on the heart in an extreme situation.

A third rather important physiological effect occurs when we go bathing. No matter what the temperature of the water we have a tendency to feel cold when we finally get out. This is because the surface of our body is wet. So long as the air is not saturated the moisture will be evaporated and the lower the humidity the faster that evaporation will take place. The evaporation of water requires a considerable amount of energy in the form of heat. As the most available source of heat is our own body we feel cold. If in addition there is a wind the moist air is constantly replaced by dryer air and evaporation is further speeded up, so increasing the sensation of cold. This phenomenon can be used to measure the humidity using a wet and dry bulb hygrometer which is described in a later section on page 51.

EXERCISES

5.5 Explain why the temperature of water ceases to rise after it reaches 100°C no matter how long it is boiled. What will happen if the container is left on the heat for too long?

5.6 What effect does pressure have on the boiling point of water? What problems occur when trying to make a hot drink at a high altitude?

5.7 You have often heard that machines are inefficient – that they waste energy. Does this mean that the energy is lost? Explain.

5.8 Why does freezing water release heat? Why doesn't the heat, released when water freezes to ice, cause the ice to melt again?

Condensation

Condensation is the reverse of evaporation. It normally occurs in the atmosphere due to the cooling of the air below its dewpoint which is the temperature at which the air will become saturated. With reference to figure 5.7 a parcel of air at **A** can become saturated either by cooling until the dewpoint is reached at (d) or by further evaporation of water into the air so increasing the humidity until saturation occurs at (e). Alternatively, saturation may be achieved by the mixing of two masses of air which separately are not saturated, as with samples **B** and **C**.

Condensation nuclei
Condensation does not take place easily unless there is a surface on which the vapour can condense. A good example is dew which tends to form on grass and on the leaves of plants. If the air is clean then it may cool well below the dewpoint without condensation occurring. It is then said to be supersaturated. The atmosphere, however, contains microscopic particles which can act as condensation nuclei. They include impurities such as common salt which may result from the evaporation of sea spray, sulphur dioxide from combustion or dust from volcanic eruptions or wind-blown soil.

Fig 5.7 Graph showing condensation processes

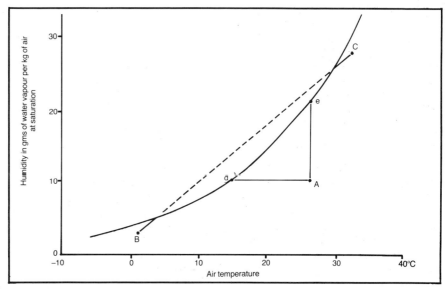

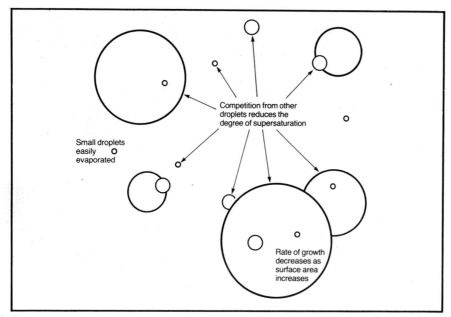

Fig 5.8   *Constraints on the growth of water droplets*

Inside figure labels:
Competition from other droplets reduces the degree of supersaturation

Small droplets easily evaporated

Rate of growth decreases as surface area increases

Salt forms a particularly good nucleus due to the fact that it is hygroscopic which means that it has an affinity for water. This is because in solution the electrically charged ions will attract water molecules. This is the same as saying that the saturation vapour pressure is less over a solution droplet than over a pure water droplet. In the case of sodium chloride nuclei, condensation has been recorded in their presence at a relative humidity of only 78 per cent.

In nature air is never free from impurities which can act as condensation nuclei. They are more numerous over the land, where on average there may be some five or six million per litre (thousand cm^3), while over the oceans there can still be as many as a million condensation nuclei per litre of air.

The growth of water droplets

Once formed, the process by which water droplets grow is far from simple and a great deal remains to be understood. To begin with, until the air is supersaturated even quite large droplets with radii up to 0.0001 mm (0.1 μm) are liable to evaporate due to the escape of fast-moving molecules. The reason for this is that the saturation vapour pressure is greater over a curved surface than over a plane surface and the greater the curvature the higher the saturation vapour pressure becomes. In these circumstances droplets with hygroscopic nuclei are more likely to survive.

On the other hand small droplets grow faster than large ones. This is because larger particles have a vastly greater surface area to add to with every increment of radius. The condensation rate is also limited by the speed at which latent heat can be released by conduction into the air around the droplet, and competition between neighbouring droplets for the available moisture

reduces the degree of supersaturation. In any case as the droplet grows the presence of the dissolved salt ceases to have much significance. For all these reasons there is a tendency for the growth rate to slow down as the droplets increase in size unless compensated for by the continued cooling of the air mass as a whole and large droplets seem to grow very slowly indeed (see figure 5.8). A radius of 0.05 mm (50 μm) seems to be the limit to growth resulting from addition by condensation.

Water droplets of this size are very little affected by gravity and remain suspended in the atmosphere. Even if droplets of radius 0.1 mm (100 μm) could be produced by condensation alone they would quickly evaporate as they fell through the unsaturated air beneath the cloud base and would be unlikely to reach the ground. For this reason true raindrops are regarded as having a radius of at least 0.50 mm (500 μm), ten times the size of the largest water droplets formed in clouds by condensation. In any case raindrops are formed in clouds in less than one hour, far too quickly to be the result of condensation alone and other processes must be sought to explain precipitation (see the last section in this chapter).

Cooling at ground level

Most forms of condensation in the atmosphere result from the air being cooled in some way. In the case of condensation at or near the ground there are three main ways in which the air may be cooled. Cooling by mixing, cooling by advection when warm air passes over a cold surface, and cooling by radiation. A number of weather phenomena result from condensation occurring at ground level, the more important of them being dew, frost and fog (figure 5.9a, b and c).

Dew

At night in the absence of insolation, the ground surface loses heat by radiation and soon becomes colder than the air above. This process is most marked on clear nights when there is no 'blanket' of cloud to keep the heat in. In time a thin layer of air in contact with the ground is cooled below the dewpoint and some of the water vapour in the air will condense to form dew. Still air also assists the formation of dew since the same air remains in contact with the ground long enough for adequate cooling to occur. A breeze will constantly change the air at ground level and if there is turbulence, bring in warmer air from above, so preventing the dewpoint from being reached.

Dew forms thickly on those objects which cool most. A spider's web is a good example because the threads have a large surface area which promotes a rapid loss of heat. Dew is always plentiful on the leaves of plants and especially so on those near the ground such as grass. This is because the air near the leaves of plants nearly always has a high humidity as a result of the process of transpiration, and so it only requires a small amount of cooling for condensation to begin.

Dew is normally heaviest in spring and autumn when there is enough warmth during the day to evaporate a good deal of moisture and when nights are still long enough to cause a relatively large drop in temperature. The ideal conditions occur after a warm day that has followed a period of heavy rain when the humidity will be especially high.

Hoar frost

The occurrence of hoar frost is promoted by the same conditions that cause dew. The difference is simply a result of the temperature falling below the freezing point of water. If the cooling is not too severe only the ground and the air immediately in contact with it will reach as low as 0°C and this causes a ground frost. An air frost occurs when the temperature of a whole layer of air near the ground also falls below freezing point.

When condensation occurs under these conditions the vapour will be thrown out directly in the form of ice crystals which grow on the pavements, the roofs and on the grass as hoar frost.

Cold air is heavier than warm air and tends to flow downhill collecting in valley bottoms and in hollows. The routeways followed by the cold air and

Fig 5.9a   Dew on a spider's web

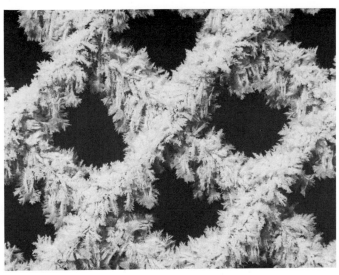

Fig 5.9b   Hoar frost

Fig 5.9c   Freezing fog on a tree

Fig 5.9d   Valley mist

Fig 5.9e   Sea fog drifting inland

the areas of low ground are therefore particularly subject to frost. As fruit trees are especially vulnerable to frost damage when in flower, the location of an orchard is critical, and a site should be chosen on sloping ground and above the level of the most frequent frosts. Orchards may also be protected by the lighting of 'smudge' fires on the windward side. These produce thick smoke which forms an artificial cloud. Thick grass also gives protection because the moisture it produces encourages dew. If condensation occurs before freezing point is reached the frost is less likely because of the latent heat which is liberated by the condensation process.

This latent heat is the reason why frozen dew is less common than one might expect. However, occasionally rain falls on to very cold ground and freezes into a continuous film of ice. This is referred to as a glazed frost and is strictly not a frost at all in the true sense.

Freezing fog is very similar and results in thick accumulations of ice on foliage and on telegraph wires which can often be brought down by the weight.

Mist
On a warm, quiet day, when the ground is wet after heavy rainfall, or where there are lakes or rivers in the vicinity there will naturally be a high humidity. During the evenings as the temperature falls wisps of mist may be seen to form over the fields and near water, especially in sheltered spots. Enclosed valleys are also places where almost calm air can be found and where the temperature is likely to fall a more than average amount. Valley mists are the result. When the next day dawns the temperature soon rises sufficiently to evaporate all the moisture and the mist quickly clears (figure 5.9d).

Fog
A mist becomes a fog when the visibility is reduced below one kilometre and as might be expected the causes are very similar.

Radiation fog results from night-time cooling under clear skies when there is little movement in the air, and is most common in Britain during winter in inland locations.

Advection fog is the result of the cooling that occurs when warm air flows over a cold surface. During the winter this can happen when warm moist air from the Atlantic Ocean flows over the cold land surface of Northwest Europe.

A similar situation exists off the coast of Newfoundland where warm air from over the North Atlantic Drift comes into contact with the cold Labrador Current. Icebergs brought down from the Greenland Coast intensify the fog around them and such a situation led to the sinking of the *Titanic*. Fogs of this kind are often referred to as sea fogs and if the wind is in the right direction they may drift in over the adjacent land areas (figure 5.9e).

Occasionally fog results from the mixing of different air masses as along an active front but these are neither common nor particularly widespread.

Stability and clouds
Clouds like fog, are composed of masses of water droplets and hill fog is really only the result of clouds forming at a low level. Unlike fog patches, however, many clouds form in air which is by no means calm and time lapse film shows that the air appears to 'boil'. It also reveals that clouds tend to grow in their central regions where there is active condensation and dissipate around their margins where mixing occurs with the dryer air that surrounds them.

As the shapes of clouds give a very good picture of the way in which the air is behaving, clouds are also good indicators of future weather and they have long been used as a simple means of weather forecasting. For example, 'mackerel sky' is associated with changeable weather, while clouds showing great vertical development indicate the likelihood of heavy rain showers in the vicinity.

Cooling by ascent
As with condensation that occurs near the ground clouds are also the result of air being cooled, but this time the cooling is a consequence of the upward movement of the air. When air ascends it undergoes expansion since atmospheric pressure decreases. The expansion of a body of air entails the increased separation of the molecules and so an increase in their potential energy. This energy must be provided in the form of heat but since the rising air mass is only surrounded by yet more air it is cut off from any external sources. The heat energy must therefore be supplied by the rising air mass itself and a fall in temperature is the result. Such a temperature change that involves no addition or subtraction of heat is termed adiabatic.

The rate of the decrease in temperature that occurs under these conditions

is 10°C per 1000 m, so long as the air remains unsaturated. This is referred to as the Dry Adiabatic Lapse Rate or DALR. However, when the dewpoint temperature is reached condensation results in cloud formation. Latent heat of condensation is released so reducing the rate at which the temperature falls. This time the temperature loss is not constant. As cooling progresses the moisture holding capacity of the air decreases and so the heat liberated, as a result of condensation, is in ever smaller amounts. Near sea level the Saturated Adiabatic Lapse Rate, or SALR, is 6°C per 1000 m but as altitude increases it gradually approaches the same value as the DALR. A rough guide is that for temperatures above 30°C the SALR is about 5°C per 1000 m rise, down to freezing point it is 6°C per 1000 m and below 0°C the rate climbs to above 7°C per 1000 m.

If a body of air should become more dense than its surroundings then it will sink. In this case it will experience increasing atmospheric pressure and the whole cooling process is reversed. The molecules of gas will move closer together and the potential energy that is lost will be converted into heat. Adiabatic warming is the result.

Temperature changes resulting from the expansion or contraction of gases are common in everyday experience. When a bicycle tyre is inflated the barrel of the pump becomes hot. This is due to the compression of the air as it is forced into the tyre. A domestic refrigerator works on a similar principle. At the back is a long folded pipe containing the gas freon. An electric motor extracts the gas from the pipe and liquifies it. This it should be noted generates heat which is allowed to escape. The liquified gas passes through a valve and drips into the other end of the pipe. As there is a very low pressure in the pipe the gas expands very rapidly and the heat required for this expansion is drawn from the freezing compartment of the refrigerator and from the food it contains.

Adiabatic changes are also demonstrated by mountain winds such as the Chinook in the Canadian Rockies and the Föhn in the Alps. These are warm winds which in the case of the Chinook, allows the cultivation of wheat in the Peace River District, further north than is usually possible, due to an early thaw in Spring.

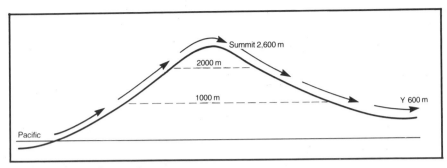

Fig 5.10 The Chinook

EXERCISES

Figure 5.10 shows air passing over a mountain range.

5.9 If the starting temperature and the humidity of the air are 20°C and 70 per cent and the dewpoint temperature is 14°C calculate:
(i) The height at which the air will become saturated (DALR 10°C per 1000 m).
(ii) The temperature of the air as it crosses the summit at 2,600 m (SALR 6°C per 1000 m).
(iii) The temperature at **Y**, 600 m above sea level.
(iv) The temperature of the air if it could return all the way to sea level again.
5.10 Explain how the release of latent heat contributes to these temperature changes.
5.11 On a copy of the diagram, mark in the cloud base, and show where you would expect rain to fall.
5.12 Explain why there is a 'rain shadow' in the lee of these mountains. What does the term 'rain shadow' mean?

Stability and instability
It has now been established that the temperature changes that are responsible for the formation of clouds are due to rising air, but why should air rise and fall? The case of the Chinook wind suggests that high ground is one cause but clouds do not only form over hills and some more general cause is needed.

As the temperature of air rises it will expand and so become less dense. If air is warmer than its surroundings then it will be lighter and so have a tendency to rise. Conversely if it is cooler it will be heavier and so have a tendency to sink. We already know that air which is rising or falling experiences temperature changes itself. These may result in the

air returning to the same temperature as its surroundings when it is said to be stable, or becoming increasingly warmer than its surroundings when it is said to be unstable.

As the adiabatic temperature changes are fixed, the stability or instability of the air must depend on its moisture content, and therefore on its ability to liberate latent heat, and on the change of temperature with altitude in the environment. As a knowledge of the stability of the atmosphere is vital for accurate weather forecasting, it is necessary to know the temperature and

Fig 5.11 Air mass stability

humidity of the air at different levels in the atmosphere. This information is obtained by means of balloons called radio-sondes. They carry a package of electrical instruments which record the pressure, temperature and humidity of the air through which they pass. These radio-sondes ascend to great heights and a ground station receives signals from the transmitter carried by the sonde and decodes them. From the information received meteorologists can plot graphs showing the temperature changes with height, and these changes are known as the Environmental Lapse Rate or ELR.

The relationships between the adiabatic and environmental lapse rates are absolutely fundamental to an understanding of air mass stability. They help to account for the height and shapes of the clouds and give an indication of the likelihood of precipitation. As the figures are more easily comprehended in the form of a diagram they are plotted on graphs known as tephigrams, an example of which is shown in figure 5.12. On it vertical

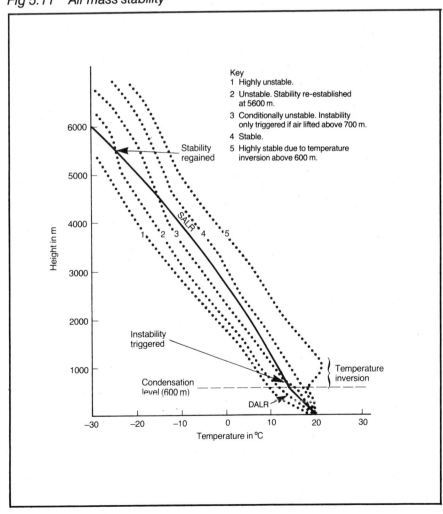

lines will be isotherms and horizontal ones pressure levels which are directly related to altitude. Sloping upwards from right to left are pecked lines which show the adiabatic temperature changes. The straight lines are dry adiabats and show the rate at which rising, unsaturated air will cool, while the curved lines are wet adiabats which show the slower rate of cooling of rising saturated air.

Temperature-height diagrams are very valuable aids to understanding the various situations that can arise in the atmosphere. Figure 5.11 illustrates a series of possibilities. Generally speaking the adiabatic lapse rates are subject to only small variations and so the diagram employs only one air mass whose ascent is shown by the continuous line. The pecked lines show five different environmental situations.

In the first case the loss of temperature with height is very rapid and the rising bubble of air is always warmer than its surroundings. This is a situation where the air is highly unstable, and it does not reach stability again until a height of over 6000 m is reached. The second case is very similar and the diagram shows that stability is regained at a height of about 5,600 m.

In case number four the ascending air is always cooler than its surroundings and so there will be no tendency for it to rise, while in case number five the temperature of the environment actually increases with altitude for a while. Such a temperature rise is called an inversion and results from cooling at ground level on a clear night, or above a cloud layer as here. In this situation it is unlikely that the rising air will ever become heated enough to be able to penetrate the inversion and so the air cannot rise more than a few hundred metres or so.

Case number three is known as conditional instability. Here the ascending air is only marginally cooler than its surroundings and it only requires a small temperature rise, or uplift over higher ground, to carry it above 700 m where it will become unstable and continue to rise under its own volition. In this case instability is conditional on some trigger mechanism coming into operation.

Figure 5.12 represents an ascent from an inland station at 0600 hours on a winter's day and illustrates some of the situations that can arise. Three inversions are shown on this ascent. The highest is the tropopause at 12,500 m and forming an ultimate limit to insta-

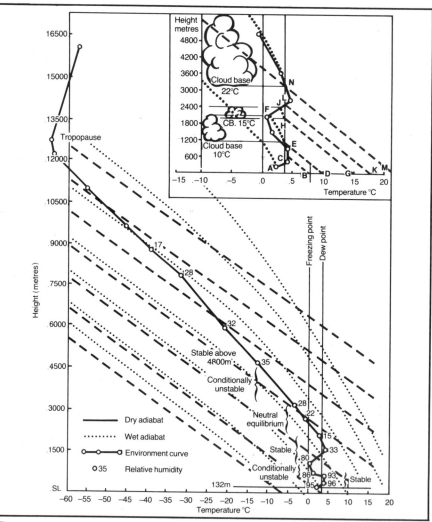

Fig 5.12 *Sample ascent plotted on simplified tephigram (temperature-height diagram). Inset shows conditions below 4800m in greater detail.*

bility. The second is a surface inversion and the result of night-time cooling, while the third is due to air subsiding under anticyclonic conditions and being warmed adiabatically and is clearly indicated by the low values of relative humidity in the air above the inversion.

It can readily be seen that there is no possibility of free convection in the air at the time of the ascent. The enlarged inset shows that air rising from **A** will be below the dewpoint temperature and cool at the SALR. It will, however, remain cooler than its surroundings at all times and so sink back to ground level. If the air could be heated to 8°C, 6°C more than at **A**, it could still only rise about 600 m before it reached the inversion at **C**, and would remain stable throughout. At **D**, 8°C warmer than at ground level, it would rise at the DALR and penetrate the inversion. At **E** the dewpoint would be reached and cloud would form at about 1,200 m, but stability is regained at **F** at the upper inversion. An ascent from **G** starting at 15°C

would result in a cloud base at **H** at about 2000 m but stability is once more attained at **J**, 400 m higher. No cloud will form at all if the rising air starts at a temperature of 18°C because the air will become stable at the dewpoint. Finally an ascent from **M** starting at 22°C penetrates the upper inversion at **N** and cloud again forms, this time with a base at 3,200m.

Cloud formation

As clouds are a result of the vertical motion of air it is possible to group them according to the mechanism by which the air is lifted as follows:

(a) Clouds due to ascent over an orographic barrier.

(b) Clouds due to gradual uplift of air over a wide area in a frontal system.

(c) Clouds due to uplift by mechanical turbulence (forced convection).

(d) Clouds due to thermal convection on a local scale.

Some cloud types will occur in more than one of these groups, however, and the internationally adopted classifica-

Group	Height of Base	Type		Description
High clouds	6,000 m to 12,000 m	Cirrus	Widespread ascent often frontal	Detached featherlike clouds with delicate fibrous structure. Clouds cast no shadow. White wisps of cloud spaced at random indicate fair weather – bands of cloud indicate the approach of a frontal system.
		Cirrocumulus		White clouds without shadows. Often arranged in bands, or in layers containing ripples. Referred to as a mackerel sky.
		Cirrostratus		A thin white veil of cloud covering the whole sky, and giving it a milky appearance. The outlines of the sun and moon are clear and have a halo. Often heralds the approach of a warm front.
Medium clouds	2,000 m to 6,000 m	Altocumulus		A white-grey layer containing flattened globular masses which may be arranged in bands or waves. There may or may not be shadows.
		Altostratus		A greyish sheet with little variation. The sun is barely visible through it. Occasional drizzle.
Low clouds	Ground level to 2,000 m	Stratocumulus	Cooling near ground	A grey-white patchy sheet or with soft grey rounded masses. Often a regular pattern such as long rows.
		Nimbostratus		Thick dark grey layer. Persistent rain or snow, sometimes heavy.
		Stratus		Grey uniform layer. Drizzle or light rain frequent.
		Cumulus	Convection due to heating from below	Detached cloud masses with horizontal base and 'cauliflower' shaped tops. Sometimes more broken and ragged in appearance and may develop vertically. Showers possible.
Clouds of great vertical extent	Up to 12,000 m	Cumulonimbus		Great rounded masses of cloud heaped up and with extensive vertical development. Dark grey but lighter at the margins. Upper parts more fibrous with flattened top to form anvil. Heavy showers and thunderstorms.

The term 'Cirrus' and the prefix 'Cirro' indicate high cloud. 'Alto' indicates medium cloud. 'Cumulus' and 'Cumulo' indicate a heap cloud arising from convectional activity. 'Stratus' and 'Strato' indicate a layer-cloud.

Fig 5.13   A classification of clouds

tion of clouds is based on their general shape and their altitude. This classification is summarised in figure 5.13. In simple terms they fall into two main categories, namely those that form under stable conditions and those that form under unstable conditions.

Cloud forms in unstable air
Cumuliform clouds are most common on hot summer days when the ground becomes warm. The sun heats the ground in an irregular way depending on whether the slopes face towards or away from the sun and on the nature of the surface: bare soil, urban areas, or woodland. Gradually a film of warm air develops near the ground and the Environmental Lapse Rate increases. Eventually bubbles of air begin to break away from the surface and travel upwards. These bubbles of warm air are known as thermals (see figure 5.14).

To begin with the rising bubbles of air are unsaturated, but they are being cooled adiabatically all the time and eventually they reach the dewpoint temperature and condensation begins. The level at which this takes place forms the cloud base and its height is largely determined by the humidity of the bubbles as they leave the ground. High humidities mean a low cloud base because less cooling is required for the dewpoint to be reached.

The size and shape of the resulting clouds depends on a number of factors. If the air through which the bubbles rise is fairly dry then mixing around the margins of the clouds causes rapid evaporation of the water droplets. Consequently the growth of the cloud is slowed down and as evaporation causes cooling, the outer layers of the cloud begin to subside thus inhibiting vertical development.

A more definite limit to vertical growth is set by the level at which the rising air once more becomes stable. In figure 5.15, diagram (a), the dewpoint is reached at 1,600 m but stability is regained at 2,200 m and so the cloud layer is relatively thin. In diagram (b) the dewpoint is reached at 2000 m but stability is not regained until well over 4000 m resulting in clouds of great vertical development. The combination of a dry environment and a narrow zone of instability will result in rather flat clouds or in no clouds at all, while a deep zone of instability and a very humid environment will cause very active cloud development indeed.

Time is a third factor in the development of cumulus cloud. As the day progresses and the sun gains in power so the ground gets warmer. The sky will remain clear, however, until the convective activity is strong enough for thermals to begin to reach the condensation level. At first small, puffy, fair weather cumulus clouds punctuate the sky and the day continues to be sunny. The scientific name for these clouds is Cumulus fractus. Further heating increases the instability and the clouds grow in size and vertical development, becoming first of all Cumulus mediocris and then Cumulus congestus. There are now only sunny intervals and during the afternoon the weather may well become thundery.

At this stage the tops of the clouds may be reaching heights of over 8000 m where the temperatures may be as low as –20°C and most of the water turns to ice. This results in fibrous cirriform cloud and the whole cloud structure is now known as cumulonimbus. Again

Fig 5.14   The development of cumulus clouds

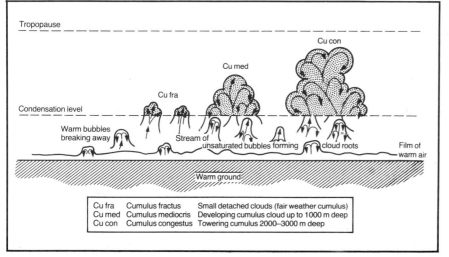

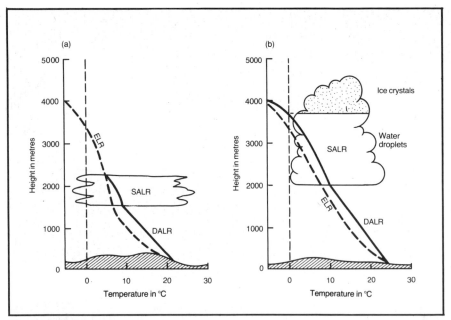

Fig 5.15   The vertical extent of clouds

oping in the base of a cumulonimbus cloud replacing the old convection cell which has spread out in anvil form, or from high level winds which cause the upper part to spread out in layers of stratus.

Clouds in stable air
Stratiform clouds are associated with a stable atmosphere, and with widespread cooling due to uplift over a large area, or to the passage of warm moist air over a cold surface. In general they have limited depth compared with their horizontal extent and are accompanied by comparatively feeble air currents.

As shown by figure 5.17 most stratus cloud is formed by advection and is very similar to fog. The cloud base is seldom above 500 m and winds are usually responsible for lifting the masses of condensed water droplets off the ground. Quite often this occurs when moist sea air spreads inland over a cold surface. The greater 'roughness' of the land compared with the sea

there are a number of different forms some of which are shown in figure 5.16. An early one is Cumulonimbus capillatus in which the filaments of cirrus first begin to break out of the top of the cloud. Eventually the cloud development may reach the tropopause at a height of 11,000 m. As the temperature ceases to fall with altitude at this level the air soon becomes stable and the cloud develops the typical flattened top or anvil which we associate with cumulonimbus cloud. Other variations result from new convection cells devel-

Fig 5.16   The development of cumulonimbus clouds

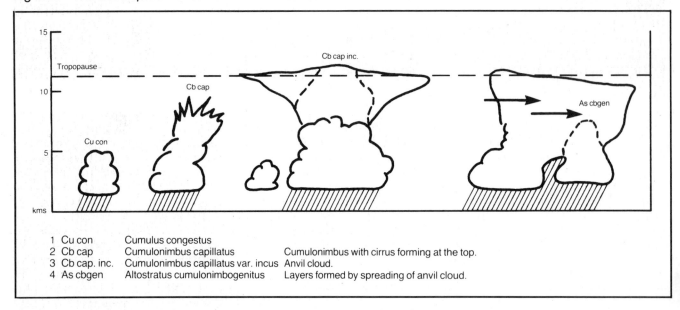

1 Cu con	Cumulus congestus	
2 Cb cap	Cumulonimbus capillatus	Cumulonimbus with cirrus forming at the top.
3 Cb cap. inc.	Cumulonimbus capillatus var. incus	Anvil cloud.
4 As cbgen	Altostratus cumulonimbogenitus	Layers formed by spreading of anvil cloud.

Fig 5.17   Cloud development in stable air

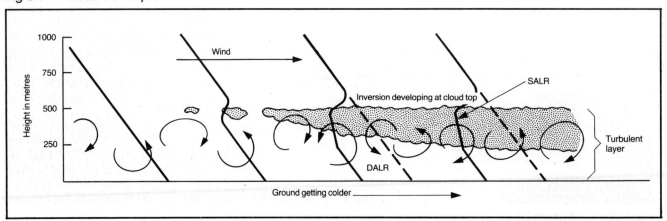

24

Fig 5.18a   Fair weather cumulus or cumulus fractus

Fig 5.18b   Cumulus congestus

Fig 5.18c   Cumulonimbus

Fig 5.18d   Stratocumulus

Fig 5.18e   Altocumulus

Fig 5.18f   Cirrocumulus

Fig 5.18g   Stratus

Fig 5.18h   Cirrus

Fig 5.18j   Cirrostratus with halo

Fig 5.18k   Lightning from cloud to cloud and cloud to earth

results in increased turbulence and the formation of a layer of stratus cloud.

Stratus cloud forms a rather monotonous grey sheet but similar conditions can give rise to cloud with a greater degree of structure. In a high pressure system the air is gently subsiding over a wide area. As it sinks it is warmed adiabatically but it seldom reaches ground level due to turbulence in the lowest layers of all caused by surface friction. An inversion is set up in the boundary zone between the subsiding air and the mixed surface layer. Stratocumulus is typical of these conditions and if the convection is cellular in character as in figure 5.17 then the familiar mackerel sky will result.

Finally thick stratiform clouds are associated with fronts and may give widespread and persistent rain. As the front approaches high cirrostratus cloud appears, followed by ever thicker layers of altostratus and nimbostratus. In complex frontal systems combinations of these clouds are likely to occur. (See figure 5.18 for examples of cloud formation.)

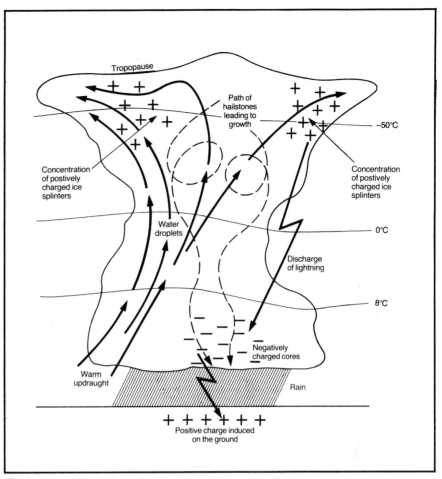

Fig 5.19   A large thundercloud

Precipitation – the formation of raindrops

Condensation alone cannot account for the growth of water droplets with a diameter greater than 0.1 mm (see *Condensation* on page 18), and in any case the process is so slow that the production of larger drops would not reach completion in the life of a cumulus or cumulonimbus cloud. Droplets of this size are not heavy enough to overcome the resistance provided by the air even when no thermals are present and so must remain in the cloud. Even if they could fall to earth they would almost certainly evaporate long before reaching the ground.

The Bergeron Process

The Swedish meteorologist Bergeron was the first to suggest that ice crystals might play a part in the formation of raindrops. The so-called Bergeron Process requires temperatures below – 20°C when ice crystals begin to grow. They form around special freezing nuclei, such as the clay mineral kaolinite, which encourages early freezing.

As the temperature in the cloud falls, ice crystals and supercooled droplets co-exist. The saturation vapour pressure, however, is less for ice than for water and when the vapour pressure in

the cloud is too low for water droplets to continue to grow by addition of condensation they start to evaporate. Meanwhile vapour continues to condense on to the ice crystals which therefore grow at the expense of the water droplets. Eventually the ice crystals splinter giving rise to an increased number of freezing nuclei.

At – 40°C supercooled droplets freeze rapidly and if the air currents are not too strong they form loose aggregates. If the air is turbulent, however, then hard pellets of ice form instead. The former are snowflakes while the latter are referred to as graupel. When they are big enough they will begin to fall from the cloud to arrive at ground level as snow or hail. Often melting will occur as they fall and both will give rise to rain, while sleet is an intermediate form that occurs in near-freezing surface air.

Hail is more common in summer when the sun is powerful enough to set up large convection storm clouds. The turbulence not only favours the formation of hail but the strong updraughts of air enable the hailstones to grow much larger before they fall, resulting in the typical summer downpours. Sleet and snow are much more commonly associated with stable conditions when cloud forms over a cold surface or in frontal systems.

Thunderstorms

Thunderstorms provide some of the most dramatic evidence of atmospheric activity and they involve an immense amount of energy. They are especially important in the tropics and in continental areas of mid-latitudes. Heavy falls of hailstones are typical of the mid-latitude thunderstorm and in the interior of a continent stones the size of golf-balls are not uncommon, and the largest known are about the size of a tennis-ball! The size is related to the number of times the hailstone is carried up and down inside the cloud. The result is that many hailstones are composed of layers of ice some of which are finely crystalline and opaque and some of which are much coarser and clear.

A typical thunderstorm is really a group of convective cells forming a series of vigorous chimneys of rising air. Each cell may be 1–5 km across and may persist for up to one hour. Once the storm has been established each cell will be replaced as it declines in activity by new cells developing around the margins. The release of latent heat helps to provide the energy which fuels the storm and as a result it may survive well into the night and long after the solar radiation which gave it birth has ceased to arrive.

The electrical activity associated with thunderstorms is now thought to be the process by which the electrical charge that is leaked into the atmosphere is returned to earth. Figure 5.19 shows how supercooled water droplets are carried up to levels where the temperature is below $-20°C$ and they begin to freeze from their surface inwards. The cold outer surfaces become positively charged with H^+ ions and the warmer cores negatively charged with OH^- ions. Continued freezing results in the expansion of the cores of the hailstones and eventually they shatter. The positively charged splinters from the shells are thought to be carried upwards while the larger negatively charged cores fall to the base of the cloud. At the same time as the charge in the cloud becomes separated a positive charge is induced in the ground below and when there is sufficient potential difference between the upper and lower part of the cloud, and between the cloud and the surface of the earth a discharge takes place causing a flash of lightning.

The Simpson and Mason Theory
Alternative ideas on the formation of raindrops were put forward in the 1930s by Sir George Simpson and B.J. Mason. Their theory depends on the great variety in the size of water droplets in clouds. Uniformly small droplets will tend to move at the same speed in a cloud but if they are mixed with larger, slow moving droplets that have formed around hygroscopic nuclei then this will encourage collisions and the amalgamation of drops. A modification of these ideas due to Langmuir points out that the terminal velocities of falling droplets are directly related to their diameters. The larger drops might therefore overtake the smaller ones and so collide with them. Alternatively the small droplets might be swept into the wake of larger ones and so absorbed. The minimum size for these larger droplets would be about 19 μm and they might result from the presence of giant nuclei or from seeding by ice crystals from higher levels within the cloud.

Other theories have suggested that differently charged droplets might coalesce as a result of electrical attraction but the separation of the drops seems in practice to be too great and the electrical charges too small. Differences in the temperatures of neighbouring droplets could also cause the warmer droplets to evaporate so providing vapour for continued condensation on the surfaces of the colder droplets; however, except for some tropical clouds the air temperatures seem to be too low for this to occur.

EXERCISES

5.13 Trace the energy changes that take place in the evaporation and condensation of water.
5.14 Condensation can be a serious problem in houses. Find out the main causes and what damage can result. What practical measures can be taken to reduce condensation in a house?
5.15 Choose a small area which possesses a good variation in aspect, vegetation and surface material including buildings. Over a period record variations in:
(i) The heaviness of dew formation.
(ii) The concentration of hoar frost.
(iii) The length of time snow lies.
Try to explain the variations you observe.
5.16 What is an adiabatic process?
5.17 What is the main cause of condensation in the atmosphere?
5.18 Water vapour (gas) changes state to form clouds (liquid) in the atmosphere. How might this affect the temperature of the surrounding air? Explain.

6 Circulation of the atmosphere

Relative motion

The movement of the earth through space is something of which we are largely unaware due to the fact that there is no stationary object available by which we can judge our relative motion. We can appreciate the situation better by reference to a journey by train.

While the train is in motion, stationary objects such as buildings and trees pass by the window, and from this we can judge the direction and speed of travel. Likewise at a station there is no motion and the unchanging view of the platform and station buildings tells us we are at rest. However, we are probably all familiar with the odd sensation produced by the movement of a nearby train which leads us to think we have resumed our journey. It comes as something of a shock to realise that we are not moving at all but that it is the other train which is in motion. Thus, on the earth, trees, buildings and people all move together and so we appear to be at rest.

In general the atmosphere also moves with the earth and a moment's thought will soon demonstrate that this is so. The earth is 40,000 km in circumference at the equator and as it rotates once every 24 hours the ground surface in the equatorial zone must travel towards the east at a little over 1,600 km per hour. If the atmosphere did not move with the earth the result would be constant winds of 1,600 km per hour in the vicinity of the equator!

Winds

While it is true that in general the atmosphere participates in the earth's rotation there exists much local variation and we experience the relative motion of the air as wind. This motion of the air occurs on many different scales but all result principally from the unequal heating of the atmosphere by solar radiation.

On a planetary scale we have the major wind belts such as the Trade Winds which greatly influenced the routes chosen by sailing ships that were incapable of sailing into the wind. These winds are largely due to the difference in heating between the equatorial regions and the poles and the large scale convection cells that are set up as a result, but they are also strongly influenced by the disposition of the continents and the differential heating of the atmosphere over land and sea.

Within these belts are winds associated with major weather systems such as tropical hurricanes or mid-latitude depressions. These large-scale systems may be more than 1,500 km across and they play a major role in the exchange of heat between the equatorial regions and the poles. On a smaller scale there are winds associated with local thunderstorms which develop as a result of the unequal heating of the earth's surface especially over the land. These may be only a few miles across and are therefore extremely local in their effects. Other local winds result from the uneven nature of the earth's surface, and in uplands there may be a strong rotary action in the movement of the air.

Smaller still are whirlwinds or twisters as they are sometimes called in the USA. Small ones do occur in Britain and a headstone in the graveyard of St Lawrence's church in Reading commemorated a man killed by a whirlwind on the platform at Reading General Station. Similar but even smaller are dust devils capable of picking up light objects such as camping gear and carrying them several yards, while the smallest of all are tiny gusts of wind which under certain conditions reveal themselves by making patterns only a foot or so long across the smooth surface of a lake.

Throughout this discussion two common themes should be noticed: the vital role of solar radiation in heating the surface of the earth which in turn heats the atmosphere from below, and the fact that winds tend to follow curved paths as illustrated by the spiral courses of winds around the centres of weather systems.

Air pressure and winds

The cause of winds is the variation in air pressure that results from the unequal heating of the atmosphere. Maps showing the distribution of pressure over the earth's surface employ lines called isobars joining places with equal pressure. They can be interpreted very like contours with areas of high pressure appearing as 'high ground' and areas of low pressure as 'low ground' (see figure 6.1).

As pressure remains constant along an isobar it follows that the direction of most rapid change of pressure must be at right angles to the isobars. The spacing of the isobars indicates the rate of change of pressure, known as the pressure gradient, and the closer the isobars the more rapid the change. This is very similar to the concept of slope on a contour map and so where the isobars are packed closely together we refer to a steep pressure gradient. Again, as acceleration down a slope increases the steeper it gets, so winds increase in strength the steeper the pressure gradient becomes.

A third similarity between isobars and contours is in their ability to reveal shape, and as the parallel is so close we

Fig 6.1 An isobaric map

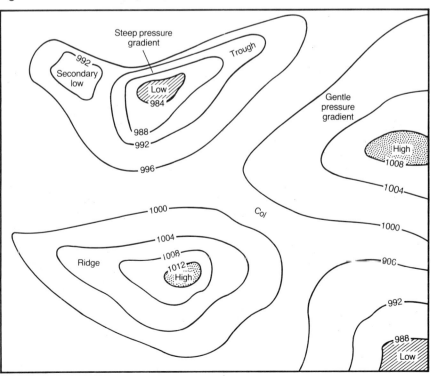

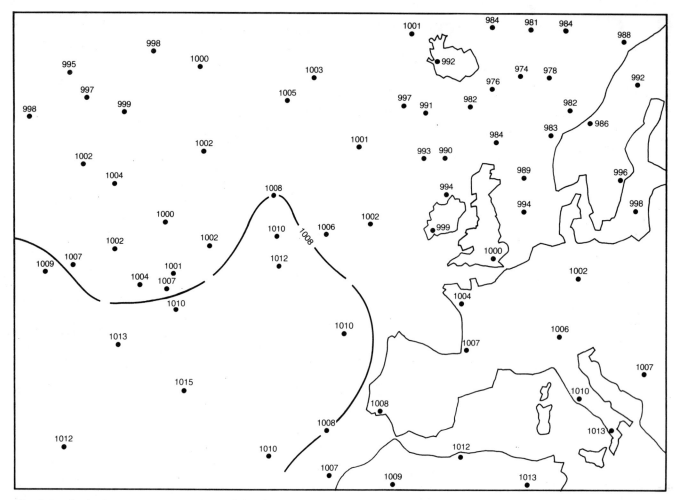

Fig 6.2   An isobaric map of the North Atlantic

often use the same word to describe the resulting feature. Thus a long, narrow area of high pressure or of high ground is referred to as a 'ridge', while a 'col' is a lower area between two hills or an area of lower pressure between two areas of higher pressure (see figure 6.1).

The interpolation of isobars
The plotting of isobaric maps depends on access to pressure readings from a network of weather stations on the land and from ships at sea. These readings marked on a map give a scatter of known values similar to the spot heights on a relief map. The 'dead ground' between the known points can now be filled in by drawing isobars using a process called interpolation.

First a suitable pressure interval is chosen, usually 4 mb, and then points of equal value at that interval are joined to produce the isobars. However, it is unlikely that many of the available pressure readings will coincide with the values chosen for the isobars which must therefore be drawn between the scatter of known points. The pressure gradient between any two points is assumed to be even and the distance is then divided proportionately. Thus the 1004 mb isobar will run halfway between the values of 1002 mb and 1006 mb but only a quarter of the

distance between the values of 1003 mb and 1007 mb. Using this method the whole isobaric pattern may be completed but it should be noted that, as with contours, isobars of different values cannot join nor can they ever intersect. It is also a good idea to plot isobars at an interval of 8 mb to begin with and then fill in the intermediate values when the approximate shape of the pressure pattern has been determined.

EXERCISES

6.1 Complete the map shown in figure 6.2 by interpolating isobars at intervals of 4 mb (the 1008 mb isobar has been drawn as an example).

6.2 Using the isobaric pattern as a guide, attempt to locate the positions of any fronts and add them to the map. (See sections on *Weather systems,* p38, and *Weather maps,* p54).

6.3 Locate on the map examples of the following:

(i) An anticyclone (high pressure centre).

(ii) A depression or cyclone (low pressure centre).

(iii) A steep pressure gradient.

(iv) A gentle pressure gradient.

(v) A ridge of high pressure.

(vi) A col.

Models of the earth's atmospheric circulation

Convection cells
Circulation within a fluid by convection can easily be demonstrated in a laboratory. If a glass tank is filled with water and a bunsen burner put under one end, the water above the flame will be warmed, and will therefore expand. Being lighter as a result, the warm water will rise to the surface and spread out, while at the same time be replaced at depth by cool, dense water spreading along the bottom from the other end of the tank (see figure 6.3). The warm surface water will lose heat as it moves away from the heat source and eventually sinks at the far end of the tank thus setting up a convection cell. The circulation of the water can be reinforced by placing ice in the water at the cool end, so creating a heat sink. If potassium permanganate crystals are also placed in the water they will dissolve producing a purple colour which circulates with the water so revealing the convection cell.

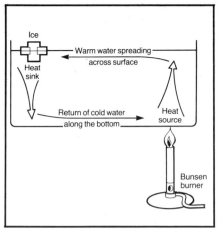

Fig 6.3   A convection cell

A very similar situation exists in a room with a fireplace along one wall and windows along the opposite wall. The fire in the grate becomes a heat source and the open windows the heat sink, and the air will circulate accordingly so distributing the heat and providing ventilation.

Simple convection models for the atmosphere

For the earth the polar regions represent heat sinks and the equatorial zone a heat source, and figure 6.4 shows the locations of the earth's warmest and coldest regions. This should result in a convection cell in each hemisphere. The air can be envisaged as sinking at the poles and spreading outwards across the earth's surface, rising at the equator and once more converging on the poles at altitude (see figure 6.5). This model, however, takes no account of the earth's rotation and so bears little relation to reality. Men have long been aware of the three major wind belts in each hemisphere, and the gradual explora-

tion of the world using sailing ships led to a considerable familiarity with the Trade Winds of the tropics, the Westerlies of mid-latitudes and the Polar Winds of high latitudes. Accounting for this pattern was not such an easy task.

The existence of a global convection system and its connection with the tropics as a heat source was suggested by George Hadley in 1735, and George Ferrel used similar ideas in his studies of cyclonic activity in the westerly winds of mid-latitudes published in 1889. The ability to connect the two systems, together with the polar winds, however, depends on a knowledge of the coriolis force and its effect on the atmospheric circulation.

The coriolis force is a result of the earth's rotation on its axis and it causes the single theoretical convection cell in each hemisphere to break up into three. The two located in the tropics and in the polar region can be regarded as direct convection cells driven by the tropical heat source and the polar heat sink respectively, while that in mid-latitudes can be thought of as an indirect convection cell driven by the other two. The three cells mesh together rather like a set of gear wheels as shown in figure 6.6. In recognition of their pioneer work the tropical cell is known as the Hadley Cell and the one in mid-latitudes as the Ferrel Cell.

The effect of the coriolis force on the movement of the air can now be explained. We already know that the atmosphere rotates with the solid earth

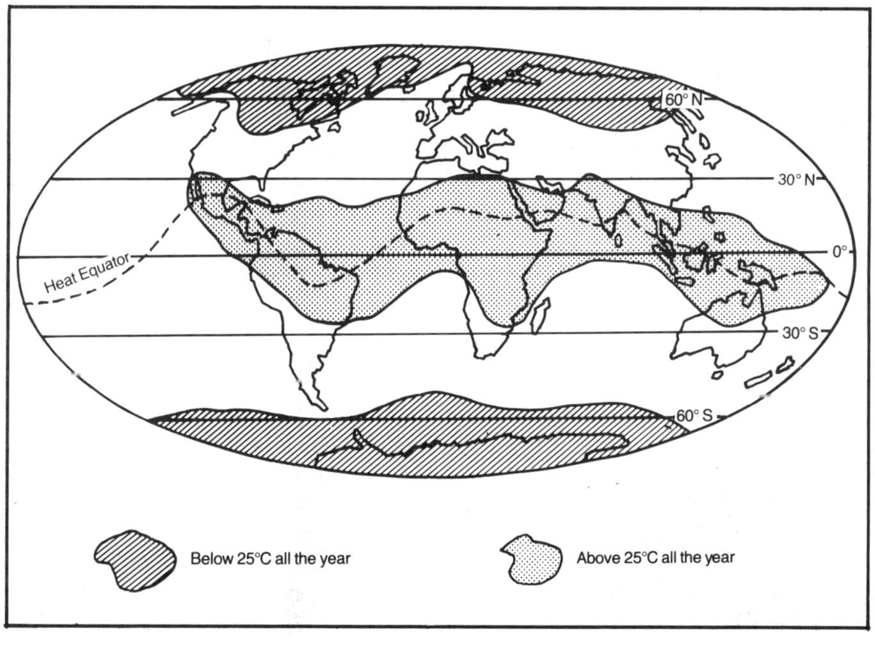

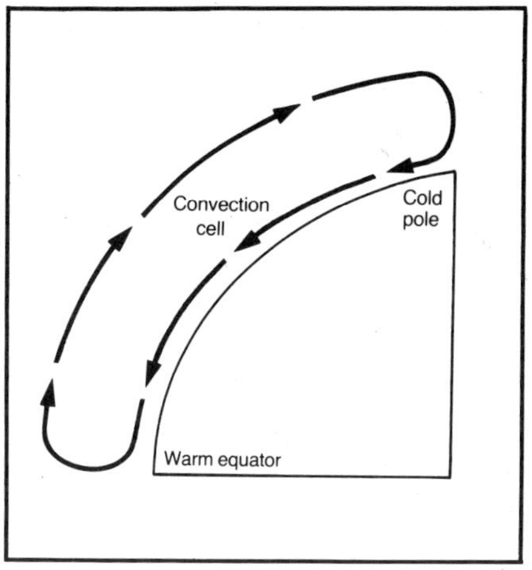

Fig 6.5   Atmospheric circulation on a non-rotating earth

and so air at the equator must travel towards the east at 1,600 km per hour. With distance from the equator, the circumference along any line of latitude decreases, so that at a distance of 60° from the equator the earth's rotational speed has been halved to 800 km per hour, while at the two poles it will be zero.

Any air stream moving equatorwards from latitude 60°N must have an eastward rotational component of 800 km per hour. As it travels towards the equator it moves into regions where the earth's rotational speed is increasing and the ground beneath begins to leave the air behind so that the flow of air must curve to the right. A similar current of air flowing towards the equator from latitude 60°S must by the same token be deflected to the left (see figure 6.7).

Air moving polewards from latitude 60°N or 60°S must encounter regions where the earth's rotational speed is decreasing and so the air will overtake the earth beneath. Again the air in the northern hemisphere must curve to the right and that in the southern hemisphere to the left as a result of the coriolis force.

Fig 6.4   The earth's warmest and coldest regions

Fig 6.6   Atmospheric circulation on a rotating earth

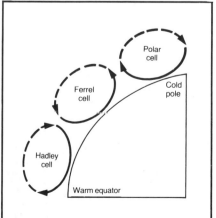

Applying these ideas to the circulation of the atmosphere shown in figure 6.8 air rising at the equator and travelling polewards aloft will be increasingly deflected to the right. By the time it has reached 30° from the equator it is no longer making any significant latitudinal progress and so air accumulates in the upper atmosphere. It has also cooled a considerable amount with the result that there is widespread subsidence giving rise to the sub-tropical high pressure zones at the earth's surface.

Descending air at the sub-tropics spreads out at ground level, much of it flowing towards the equator to complete the Hadley Cell. As it does so it curves to the right in the northern hemisphere to become the Northeast Trades and to the left in the southern hemisphere to become the Southeast Trades.

Meanwhile air moving polewards from the centres of high pressure about 30°N and 30°S of the equator is also deflected by the coriolis force to become the Westerlies. At the poles, cold, dense air also gently subsides spreading outwards at ground level. Again the air is moving latitudinally and is deflected to the right or to the left in the two hemispheres to become the polar northeasterlies or the polar southeasterlies. The result is a convergence between the polar winds and the westerlies between 50° and 60° from the equator and rising air in these latitudes encourages the formation of the centres of low pressure characteristic of these regions.

Winds of the upper air: a new model of atmospheric circulation

The study of atmospheric circulation using satellites has enabled meteorologists to construct a new model which not only corresponds more closely to observed reality, but which should enable more accurate forecasts to be made. Most important of all, it reveals that weather systems such as the mid-latitude depressions are essential parts of the atmospheric circulation and not mere interruptions of it.

The major recent discovery is the existence of powerful winds in the upper atmosphere, now referred to as jet streams. There are two in each hemisphere and they are found between the main convection cells at the sub-tropical convergences and at the polar fronts (see figure 6.9). These now need to be included in our model of the circulation of the earth's atmosphere but

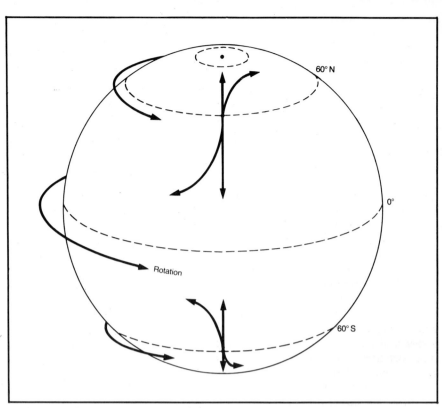

Fig 6.7   Deflection of air by the coriolis force

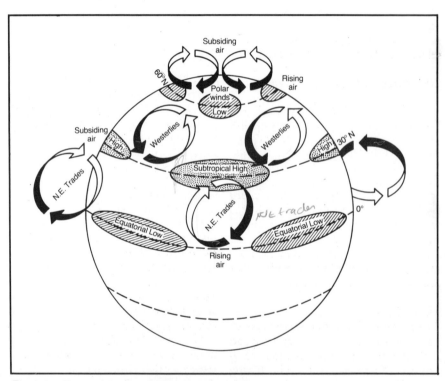

Fig 6.8   The earth's major wind belts

although meteorologists have gone a long way, our understanding is still far from complete.

The new model of the general circulation retains the three convection cells in each hemisphere but views their roles, their mode of operation and their relative importance in the global pattern rather differently.

As figure 6.9 shows, the troposphere not only gets thinner towards the poles, it is also stepped so that the tropopause is divided into three sections as well. It

appears that these breaks in the tropopause coincide with zones of rapid latitudinal temperature change in the upper air, and it is here that the powerful eastward flowing currents of air called the jet streams are located.

It is worth recalling at this point that the whole global circulation exists because of the temperature difference between the equatorial regions and the poles, and is itself the main means of transferring excess heat away from the tropics. The Hadley Cell is still held to be important in this respect, but pole-wards heat transfer in low latitudes appears to be concentrated mainly at the western ends of the sub-tropical high pressure cells, where troughs in the mid-latitude westerlies extend towards the equator. Indeed the role of the sub-tropical high pressure cells in the global circulation now seems to be one of major importance.

The existence of the other two vertical convection cells is rather more questionable. The polar anticyclones are far from permanent features of the global system, but cold dense air does move equatorwards from these icy regions, especially in winter. However, in view of the small mass of air involved its importance to the general circulation is somewhat limited.

In the mid-latitudes it is now thought that heat transfer is accomplished by horizontal circulations rather than vertical ones. The Ferrel Cell is there-fore replaced by quasi-stationary highs and the moving highs and lows near the surface, acting in conjunction with the related wave patterns in the winds aloft.

The new model explained

It is often the case that new break-throughs in science create more problems than they solve, but the period that follows when new concepts are developed, or borrowed from other fields of study, is usually an exciting one and eventually leads to a more profound understanding. It is clear that we are at present in just such a period with regard to the circulation of the atmosphere and we must now turn our attention to some of the new ideas that are current in the literature.

How winds are steered
The motion of the atmosphere depends on the existence of a driving force and the direction of that motion on a number of steering forces. The driving force (P) is the pressure gradient devel-oped across the isobars by the constant adjustment between the forces of con-vection and gravitation. The steering forces are the coriolis force (D) which results from the earth's rotation, the centrifugal force (C) and a frictional force (F).

(a) An explanation has already been given of the deflection of winds by the coriolis force, but it is useful to rein-force our understanding by comparing the behaviour of the atmosphere with that of a weight whirled around at the end of a piece of cord. The rotation of

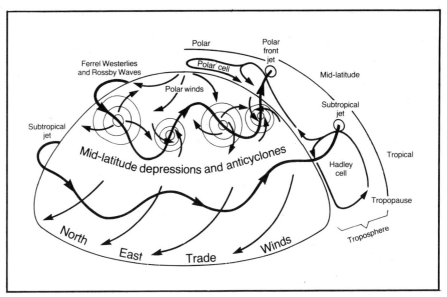

Fig 6.9   The general circulation of the atmosphere

the earth imparts angular momentum to the atmosphere and at the equator its value depends on the equatorial radius. If the air now moves polewards the radius of rotation decreases and in order to conserve angular momentum the air must move faster. This is the same as shortening the cord which again results in the weight at the end rotating more quickly. As a result the air will have an increasing rotational velocity compared to the earth the further it travels towards the pole and will therefore be deflected towards the right in the northern hemisphere and to the left in the southern hemisphere.

(b) The centrifugal force (C) acts on any body following a curved path. In reality in order to follow a curved path there must be an inward acceleration, known as the centripetal acceleration, towards the centre of rotation. For example, in order to maintain the bal-ance of forces a bicycle must be leaned into a corner when going around it.

However, it is the centrifugal force we are most aware of and in the case of the earth it is this force which creates demonstrable effects. The reduction in the value of gravity towards the equator is a result of the increase in the centri-fugal force and so the earth bulges slightly along the equator, and has a compensatory flattening at the poles.

In general the value of the force increases with the velocity and decreases with the radius of curvature. Thus the tighter the bend, and the greater the speed, the greater the force will be.

(c) The frictional force (F) only affects air near the surface of the earth, but how near depends on how rough the

surface is. For water surfaces or flat terrain a figure of 500 m is usually accepted. Its effect is to retard the air so reducing the centrifugal force which depends on velocity. As a result the pressure gradient force becomes more dominant and winds blow more and more obliquely across the isobars. The angle increases with proximity to the earth's surface and with its roughness, and averages $10° - 20°$ over the sea and $25° - 35°$ over land.

Motion in the upper atmosphere
Air in the upper atmosphere is subject to the driving force (P) and the coriolis force (D) where there are straight isobars (see figure 6.10). The coriolis force will increasingly deflect winds until they are flowing parallel to the isobars. No further deflection is poss-ible and the pressure gradient force (P) and the coriolis force (D) are now in balance. Such a balanced wind flowing along the isobars is known as a geostrophic wind. It will be noticed that when facing in the direction of flow (i.e., with your back to the wind), high pressure will be to the right and low pressure to the left in the northern hemisphere, and the reverse will be true in the southern hemisphere. This is known as Buys Ballots Law after the Dutchman of that name.

The jet stream in the sub-tropics may be regarded as such a geostrophic wind. Air rising at the equator moves pole-wards aloft and is deflected by the coriolis force. At about 30°N and 30°S a balance is achieved resulting in a strong stream of air moving from west to east in both hemispheres.

If the isobars are curved, or form

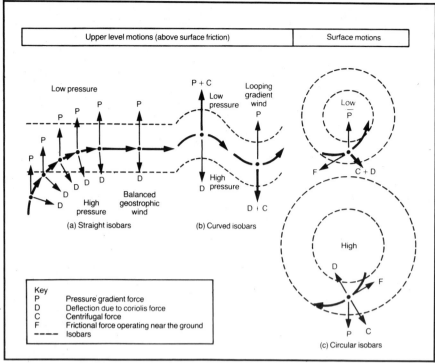

Fig 6.10   How winds are steered

Figure 6.11 shows diagrammatically a contour chart of the 500 mb surface and the 1000 mb surface. The thickness of the air layer between them is obtained by drawing lines through the intersections of the contours for the two surfaces. If we wish to obtain the direction of the thermal wind for this layer we must first mark in the gradient winds for the upper and lower surfaces. Being gradient winds these will flow parallel to the contours as shown in the diagram. Therefore the resultant wind must flow parallel to the 'thickness lines'; it is called a thermal wind because the thickness of an air layer is proportional to its mean temperature. Low thickness values imply cold air and high thickness values imply warm air. Furthermore, in the northern hemisphere, when looking downwind, cold air (low thickness) should be to the right, so obeying Buys Ballots Law.

The circumpolar vortex and the Rossby Waves

Figure 6.12 is an example of a contour chart for the upper atmosphere. The lines on the chart are contours which show the average height of the 700 mb surface in February 1958 for the northern hemisphere. The pattern produced by the contours is a simple one consisting of rings surrounding the polar region, and they indicate a strong flow of air along the contours from west to east.

waves as they often do in practice, then the centrifugal force (C) must also be considered. Reference to figure 6.10 shows that the centrifugal force acts alternately north and south supporting the pressure gradient force and the coriolis force in turn. The resulting balance sustained by these forces is not so exact as before and gives rise to a looping wind known as the gradient wind.

Air flows near the ground
Near the ground the frictional force (F) comes into play. This allows the winds to blow at a greater angle to the isobars and the rougher the terrain the more this is so. The pressure systems that develop here are therefore more cell-like and the air spirals in towards the centre of a low pressure system, or out from the centre of a high pressure system. In the northern hemisphere the direction of flow is clockwise about a centre of high pressure and anticlockwise about a centre of low pressure, and because of the coriolis force the reverse is true of the southern hemisphere. The resolution of the forces involved is shown in figure 6.10.

The roughly circular pressure systems found in mid-latitudes can therefore be explained in purely mechanical terms although differential heating at the earth's surface certainly plays a part. Pressure systems of mainly thermal origin are more typical of the lower atmosphere in tropical regions.

Contour and thickness charts
Geostrophic and gradient winds blow in slightly different directions at different levels in the atmosphere and this is

often revealed by the motion of clouds. Whole layers of air can be visualised as sliding over each other with varying velocities and directions. This gives rise to degrees of wind shear with height and so the general flow of air within any layer is averaged out and the result is simply called the thermal wind.

In order to deal with these ideas meteorologists construct maps of the atmosphere known as contour charts. In these instead of plotting the variation of pressure at a given altitude, they plot a contour map of the variation in height of a given pressure surface.

Fig 6.11   A thickness chart. G1000 and G500 are the gradient winds for the 1000 mb and 500 mb surfaces, and TR is the resultant thermal wind for the 1000 – 500 mb layer

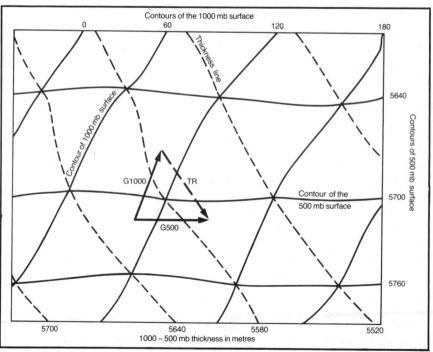

Figure 6.13 is a similar map, but this time it shows the actual situation at a precise time and uses the temperature distribution for a given pressure surface rather than its height. The pattern is very much the same but shows that some of the isotherms cluster together, thus indicating where the winds are strongest and therefore the location of the Polar Front Jet. This powerful flow of air around the pole forms the Ferrel Westerlies and is sometimes referred to as the circumpolar vortex.

The Rossby Waves
So far the air-flows in the upper and lower atmosphere of the mid-latitudes have been dealt with separately, but in fact changes in the air-flow with altitude are gradual and progressive. Furthermore the motion of the air in the lower atmosphere is profoundly influenced by what is happening aloft. For this reason studies of the upper atmosphere are not of mere academic interest.

An important feature of both the upper atmosphere charts is the existence of sinuous waves that appear in the Ferrel Westerlies. These are a more or less permanent feature of the upper westerlies and are called the Rossby Waves. They can be seen more clearly in figure 6.13 which shows that the jet stream must swing continually towards and away from the pole. Where the isotherms bulge towards the equator, as over Iceland, there are troughs of low pressure in the upper atmosphere, and where they bulge polewards, as over the British Isles and Western Europe, there are ridges of high pressure. This is shown diagrammatically in figure 6.14 with the Ferrel Westerlies forming the looping gradient wind described earlier in the chapter.

Between two and six Rossby Waves can normally be distinguished in the northern hemisphere, while three is more common in the stronger flow of the southern hemisphere. The number and position of these waves change rather slowly thus imposing a cyclic pattern on atmospheric conditions. The position of the troughs could well be influenced by heat sources such as large land masses in summer. A similar but less predictable influence may be found in the temperature of oceanic water. Changes in the location of ocean currents and in the temperature of surface water may cause changes in the wave patterns and so produce new weather sequences at the earth's surface.

The fairly stable nature of the Rossby Waves may result from the influence of

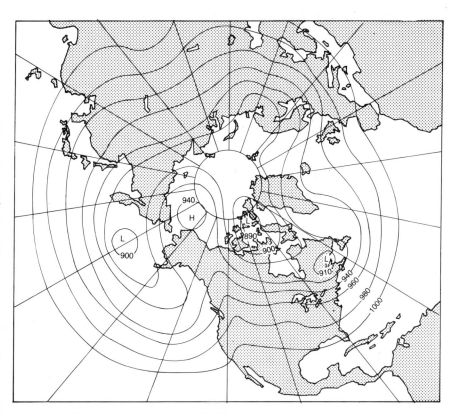

Fig 6.12   Mean 700 mb surface for February 1958

major orographic barriers such as the Andes or the Rockies. Indeed it may be that these mountain ranges are a primary cause of the Rossby Waves and that their location provides an anchorage point for the whole wave system in each hemisphere.

Vorticity
The key to understanding this lies in the relative vorticity of the air and of the rotating earth. Vorticity is the amount of spin possessed by a rotating body. For the earth vorticity is at a maximum at the poles where it is the only motion resulting from the earth's rotation on its axis. It is like a skater spinning on the ice where there is no linear motion whatsoever. At the equator, however, the earth's surface is parallel to the axis of rotation and therefore vorticity is zero. This is illus-

Fig 6.13   Temperature distribution at 500 mb surface for the northern hemisphere at 03 GMT, 6 February 1952

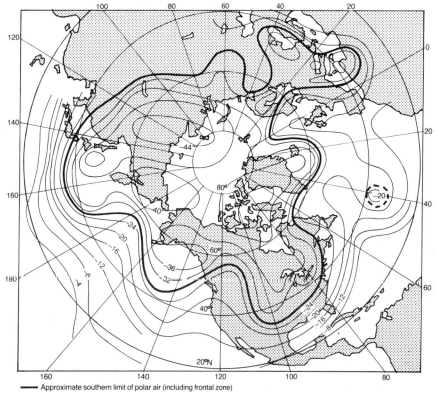

—— Approximate southern limit of polar air (including frontal zone)

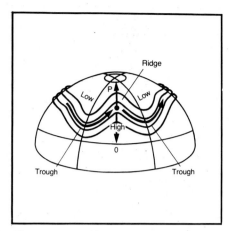

Fig 6.14   The Ferrel Westerlies

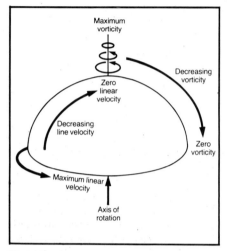

Fig 6.15   Vorticity and linear velocity on a rotating earth

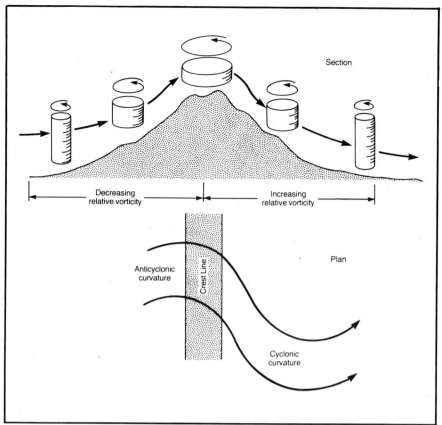

Fig 6.16   The effect of mountain barriers on the flow of the upper westerlies

trated by figure 6.15 which shows that vorticity decreases from a maximum at the pole to zero at the equator while linear velocity decreases from a maximum at the equator to zero at the pole. Thus at any point between the two extremes the motion of the earth's surface can be regarded as a combination of linear and vorticular motion.

If we imagine a pressure system approaching the Western Cordilleras of North America, the air spiralling around it will possess a degree of vorticity relative to the earth. This we can call relative vorticity. As the air crosses the crest of the mountains it is forced to contract vertically. As a result its vorticity is decreased in much the same way as that of an ice skater who revolves more slowly when she crouches down and spreads her arms. This is because angular momentum (mass × velocity × radius) is conserved, and an increase in radius is balanced by decreasing vorticity. The vorticity of the earth (global vorticity) must therefore increase relative to that of the air and the relative motion of the air becomes clockwise or anticyclonic. Once over the crest the reverse tendency sets in and the air gains in vorticity relative to the earth as it expands vertically, like

the skater, whose spin accelerates as she stands up pulling her arms in close to her sides (see figure 6.16).

The motion of the air now becomes cyclonic as it curves in an anticlockwise direction. In this way a wave is established. The air continues to move anticlockwise downstream of the mountains until it is travelling polewards once more. The earth's vorticity is now increasing again and gains on that of the air. Once global vorticity exceeds relative vorticity a clockwise or anticyclonic curvature will set in until the air is once more moving away from the pole. In this way a series of standing waves might be established. The motion of the air as it moves latitudinally constantly compensates for the changing vorticity of the earth beneath. Thus, as the air moves equatorwards it increases its relative vorticity and curves cyclonically, and as it moves polewards in the next limb of the Rossby Waves it curves anticyclonically until once more it is moving equatorwards.

The Rossby Waves and surface pressure systems

As air moves through the Rossby Waves it is subject to a changing balance of forces. While the isobars are straight the pressure gradient force and the coriolis force can reach a state of balance and a geostrophic wind results. With curved isobars the centrifugal force has also to be taken into account. For anticyclonic curvature it acts with the

pressure gradient force and winds are stronger than the spacing of the isobars would suggest. Such a wind is said to be supergeostrophic. The opposite is true for cyclonic curvature. The centrifugal force acts against the pressure gradient force and winds are lighter than the isobar spacing suggests. Such a wind is said to be subgeostrophic.

The motion of the air is therefore subject to alternate acceleration and deceleration and it can be compared with the behaviour of the cars in a familiar fairground ride. As they go round the floor rises and falls so simulating troughs and ridges. The passengers in the cars experience acceleration as they rise and deceleration as they sink. At the same time the cars, which are free to spin about a vertical axis, increase in vorticity on the ridges and decrease in vorticity in the troughs. Experience suggests that the cars tend to spin only one way, but anyone who has been rash enough to sample a ride will remember the sensation when occasionally the car goes into a reverse spin!

The result of all this is that wind speeds are greater through the ridges of the Rossby Waves than through the troughs. This means that upwind of a trough air is arriving faster than it leaves and a convergence is set up aloft. This is compensated for by subsidence and a divergence near the ground, so here we find a surface anticyclone.

In the downwind limb of the trough

the air accelerates from trough to ridge and a divergence results aloft. To compensate for this air ascends from the surface causing a convergence and therefore a low pressure area at ground level.

So long as the Rossby Waves remain stable the resulting high pressure and low pressure areas are stationary. Examples of these semi-permanent high and low pressure areas are the anticyclone in central North America and the Icelandic Low. However, as figure 6.17 shows wherever there are northbound divergent streams of air in the upper atmosphere, surface low pressure systems are encouraged and such a situation is described as cyclogenic. Likewise southbound convergent airstreams promote surface high pressure systems and so can be thought of as anticyclogenic.

The zonal index

Thus changes in the position and number of the Rossby Waves may be used to account for changes in the pattern of weather experienced at the earth's surface. Long term weather sequences such as the wet summer of 1973 or the unusually dry one of 1976 in Britain are certainly strongly influenced by the disposition of warm or cold water at the ocean surface, for this can tie the wave pattern down for a long period of time. Short term sequences lasting a few weeks only are more likely to be due to smaller changes in the shape and pattern of the waves.

Figure 6.18 shows a common sequence of changes. At first there is a strong westerly flow with only poorly developed waves. This latitudinal flow over the British Isles brings highly unsettled weather with a rapid succession of depressions separated by ridges of high pressure. Under these conditions there will be a strong pressure gradient across the upper westerlies giving a high zonal index.

As time passes waves begin to form and increase in amplitude so that winds tend to blow along the meridians giving meridional flow. The pressure difference with latitude is now much smaller giving a low zonal index. Eventually the waves break up altogether resulting in a cellular pattern with cold lows in the south and warm highs in the north. The warm anticyclones are particularly stable and slow moving causing other weather systems to move around them. For this reason they are termed blocking anticyclones. Under these conditions weather in Britain tends to be

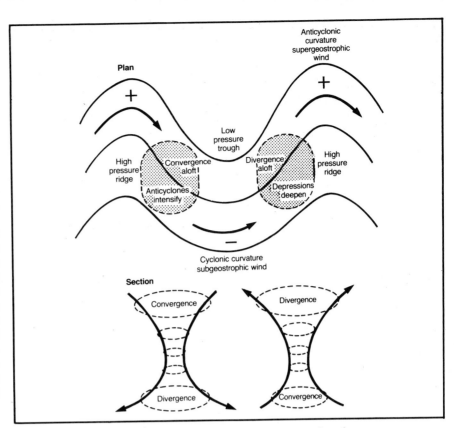

Fig 6.17 The relationship between upper air flow and surface pressure systems in mid-latitudes

dominated either by occluded cold depressions or by warm anticyclones.

Complicated as the motion of the atmosphere may be, especially in the Ferrel Cell, it is all part of the process by which heat is exchanged between the equatorial zones and the poles. Thus under low zonal conditions warm highs can be regarded as an invasion of cold polar air by warm air from the sub-tropics. Similarly in a depression warm surface air is exchanged with colder air from the upper atmosphere, while at the same time immense amounts of latent heat are released into the atmosphere by the condensation of water vapour. As the next chapter will make clear in more detail, depressions are also an essential part of the process of heat exchange in the atmosphere.

Fig 6.18 The zonal index

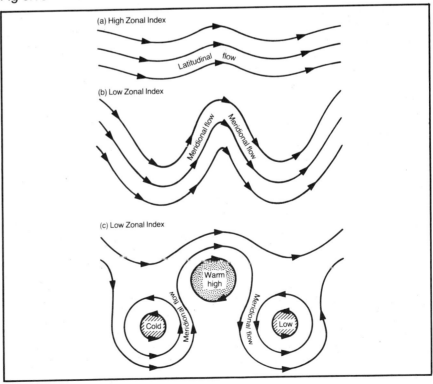

7 Weather systems

During the twentieth century, as weather stations have become more and more widely distributed throughout the world, especially in the northern hemisphere, the study of meteorology has benefitted from the availability of increasing amounts of data. This has not only allowed us to increase our understanding of the way the earth's atmosphere behaves, it has also enabled meteorologists to give increasingly accurate and detailed forecasts. At the same time the development of commercial farming, the growing volume of shipping at sea and most recently the rapid growth of the aero-space industry, has increased the demand for these forecasts and more importantly provided the finance and the technology to make them possible.

There is today perhaps no other scientific field in which the nations of the world co-operate so closely as in meteorology. The weather experienced in Britain today depends on what happened in the air over the Atlantic last week and in the water last month. Only with the help of a complete picture can we hope to get really accurate weather forecasts, and for this reason the World Weather Watch has developed, in which information is shared, and any weather service can receive anyone else's forecasts and satellite pictures.

Today there are over 7000 weather stations permanently manned by the various agencies of the World Meteorological Organisation (WMO). Of these about 4000 provide the WMO with surface observations every six hours while some 800 also take regular soundings of conditions in the upper air using radio-sondes which have been available since they were developed in the 1930s. Since 1 April 1960 when the first weather satellite was launched, we have also had the benefit of almost continuous views of the atmosphere in motion, whilst on the ground analysis of all the available data is greatly assisted by the use of powerful computers.

Even in research there is full international co-operation. In 1974, scientists from 25 nations collaborated in the Atlantic Tropical Experiment (code name GATE) using 38 ships, 3 weather ships, 13 aircraft, 15 surface and 3 radio-sonde weather stations and a geostationary satellite. This was the first of a series of experiments organised by the WMO as part of GARP, the Global Atmosphere Research Programme.

Air masses

During the first quarter of this century, as more detailed information became available, it was realised that in some parts of the world large bodies of air could be found which possessed remarkable uniformity of temperature, moisture content and vertical structure. These bodies of air became known as air masses and the zones of rapid change and mixing that lay between them were called fronts. It soon became clear that many of the day to day weather changes that occur in mid-latitudes depended on the formation and movement of the fronts between neighbouring air masses and so grew up a field of study known as air mass climatology. The ideas involved were developed during the First World War by a team of meteorologists working in Norway, and included V. and J. Bjerknes, H. Solberg and T. Bergeron; they still form the basis of most weather analysis and forecasting.

Source regions

In order to acquire sufficiently uniform characteristics an air mass must occupy a fairly uniform part of the earth's surface and be able to remain relatively undisturbed for a period of at least 3–5 days. Such regions are known as source regions and are found in areas dominated by the large semi-permanent high pressure systems. These include the sub-tropical high pressure cells such as the Azores High Pressure over the Atlantic and that over the Sahara, the interiors of large land masses such as Siberia and northern Canada in winter, and the Arctic Basin. In addition to these, central Asia and the desert states of the USA also produce great accumulations of warm, dry surface air in summer (see figure 7.1).

Air masses are now classified on the basis of two primary factors. The first is the temperature resulting in a threefold division into arctic, polar and tropical air, and the second is the character of the source region giving maritime and continental types. If these two aspects are now combined it is possible to recognise six different types of air mass as shown in figure 7.1.

When an air mass moves away from its source region it is gradually modified, but it will nevertheless retain its original characteristics for several days.

Fig 7.1 *A generalised map of source regions for air masses affecting the British Isles*

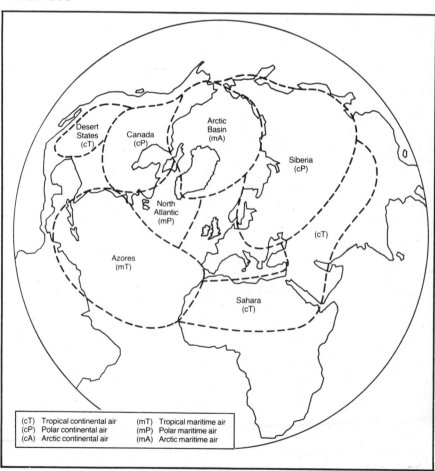

(cT) Tropical continental air   (mT) Tropical maritime air
(cP) Polar continental air   (mP) Polar maritime air
(cA) Arctic continental air   (mA) Arctic maritime air

For this reason it also carries with it distinctive weather conditions which will affect those areas that lie in its path. The British Isles in particular lie outside any recognised source region and so tend to be dominated by air masses from each of the nearby source regions in turn. Our typically changeable weather results from the fact that we lie in a region of conflict between neighbouring air masses and it is strongly influenced by the way the battle sways back and forth over our islands.

Air masses affecting the British Isles
Figure 7.2 shows the routes followed by the main air masses affecting the British Isles. As a result of our location on the eastern shores of the Atlantic Ocean in the zone of westerly winds, it will come as no surprise that our weather is largely dominated by maritime air masses.

Polar maritime (mP) air occupies these islands for about two-fifths of the year in all seasons, and comes from its source region in the North Atlantic south of Greenland. Although the temperature is fairly low it is warmed from below by its passage over the North Atlantic Drift and by the time it reaches Britain it is highly unstable. The result is considerable amounts of cumulus cloud often with a strong vertical development which produces short-lived but rather heavy showers. The strong convective activity prevents smoke or haze from accumulating and good visibility is characteristic of these showery air streams. Sometimes, however, and often after the passage of a depression, polar maritime air will take a long sea track to the south so that it approaches Britain from the southwest. In this case it will be cooled from below as it comes northward and become more stable, giving sea fog in early summer and light cloud as it moves in over a warm land surface.

Tropical maritime (mT) air comes to Britain from the southwest and dominates our weather for about one tenth of the year in all seasons. When it leaves its source region in the tropical North Atlantic it is warm and moist with clear skies and often brings this kind of weather with it to the British Isles. However, surface cooling increases the stability and may result in low stratus cloud and sea fog. Also in summer, the heating from below as it moves inland can cause strong local convection and trigger intense thunderstorms.

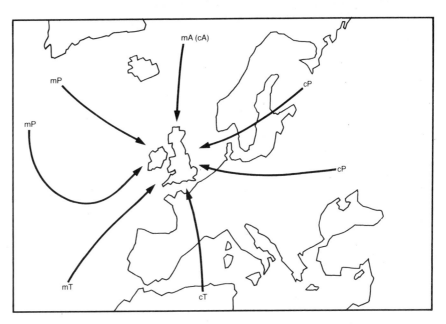

Fig 7.2   *Routes followed by air masses affecting the British Isles*

Polar continental (cP) air is far less common over Britain and usually only affects these islands from December to February. It develops in Siberia and over northern Scandinavia in winter and since it passes over a cool land surface for almost its whole journey it remains dry and brings intensely cold, clear weather to Britain. Long clear nights encourage loss of heat by radiation which causes hard frosts, and if the air is still dense fog will occur, especially inland. The passage of polar continental air across the North Sea does little to affect its temperature but it may pick up moisture to give cloudy, drizzly weather, especially along the east coast.

Arctic air rarely affects Britain but when it does it can have disastrous results. In winter, when the Arctic Ocean is frozen over, the air in the source region is designated arctic continental (cA), but the long journey over the sea allows it to be modified so that by the time it reaches Britain it is more convenient to regard it as arctic maritime (mA) air. Although very cold when it leaves the source region it has a long sea track across the North Atlantic Drift and is warmed considerably from below, so that the resulting weather in Britain is not as cold as that brought by polar continental air. Instead the air picks up a great deal of moisture and becomes highly unstable, bringing heavy snow showers, especially on northern coasts and over high ground inland.

Tropical continental (cT) air reaches Britain only very occasionally and comes from North Africa. The warm, dry air is cooled from below as it moves north and arrives in a very stable condition, bringing heat waves in summer with long sunny periods, but with a

chance of thunder in the south. Sometimes the air carries sufficient moisture picked up en route for thin stratus cloud to form, accompanied by thin drizzle and poor visibility. The rare winter incursions of tropical continental air bring unusually warm, dry weather for the time of year.

Anticyclones
Anticyclones or high pressure systems usually contain only one of the air masses described in the previous section and so are not normally associated with fronts. There are two main types of anticyclone in mid-latitudes. The first are large and slow-moving and are either poleward extensions of the subtropical high pressure cells or of continental high pressure cells, or they are blocking anticyclones produced by the break up of the wave pattern in the upper air. The second group are found interspersed between a family of depressions, and they form downstream of a ridge in the upper air where there is convergence aloft resulting in subsidence and a corresponding high pressure cell at ground level. These anticyclones are usually smaller and as they travel with the depressions they are associated with, they are far more mobile.

Atmospheric pressure increases towards the centre of an anticyclone and the subsiding air spirals outwards in a clockwise direction in the northern hemisphere. The winds are controlled by a balance of forces in which the pressure gradient force (P) and the centrifugal force (C) work together opposing the coriolis force (D). Such a balance can only be achieved if the centrifugal force and the pressure gradient force are relatively small and

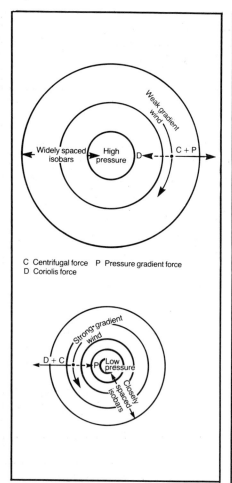

Fig 7.3 *The balance of forces around centres of high and low pressure*

Fig 7.4 *A generalised view of the main frontal zones in the northern hemisphere*

so the isobars are widely spaced and the winds tend to be light (see figure 7.3).

As the air in an anticyclone is gently subsiding it is also being warmed adiabatically which also results in a decrease in the relative humidity. For this reason cloud formation is suppressed and anticyclones are often associated with clear skies and sunny weather. In summer the result is frequently a heat wave but with sufficient cooling at night by radiation for early morning mist or 'heat haze' to occur. However, it is rare for this kind of weather to continue for long. A succession of hot sunny days will lead to a film of warm air building up at the base of the atmosphere. Eventually bubbles of warm air begin to break away from the surface and growing convective activity will lead to the development of thunderstorms (see *Precipitation* on pages 27-8).

In winter the long days are replaced by equally long nights and there is a net loss of heat at ground level. In the early evening the stars shine brightly in a clear sky and if there is a moon it will be quite light. Ground frost soon develops leading to a glistening white hoar frost. However, the stillness of the air also encourages condensation and by morning a dense fog is often the result.

This may be slow to clear especially inland and if an inversion forms above the fog, smoke and fumes are also unable to escape.

Not all anticyclones bring clear weather. Air that has moved northwards towards Britain from the Azores will have been cooled in its lower layers giving rise to a low level inversion. Heating during the day may still result in a shallow layer of instability beneath the inversion and the formation of a sheet of strato-cumulus cloud. Alternatively, beneath the subsiding air there may be a turbulent layer caused by friction with the ground beneath. Adiabatic warming above the turbulent layer may also cause an inversion resulting in a sheet of stratus cloud immediately below it. Far from producing fine, sunny weather it produces anticyclonic gloom instead and may even be accompanied by fine drizzle as well.

Fronts and frontogenesis

Very different weather is produced where two contrasting air masses are found in conflict along a front. The Atlantic Polar Front shown on figure 7.4 separates tropical maritime and polar maritime air and although both

air masses have a fairly high relative humidity there may be on average a difference of 7°C in summer and as much as 12°C in winter.

A frontal zone such as this is an area of great activity and is subject to a delicate balance which is constantly undergoing adjustment. A good illustration is provided by the electric lamps that contain two different coloured and immiscible liquids. Before the current is switched on the denser liquid lies at the bottom of the glass container and the lighter liquid on top. The light, however, generates heat at the base which should result in convective activity. For a while the surface of separation, which we can regard as a kind of front, remains stable but then begins to bulge in a rather grotesque way. The balance between the two liquids has been disturbed and the surface of separation becomes very unstable presenting a constantly changing pattern. Eventually bubbles begin to break away and rise to the surface rather as thermals do in the atmosphere.

A front is also a very unstable phenomenon. It separates air masses of different temperature and density but this time on a rotating earth. The effect of this is to replace the expected horizontal stratification by fronts that are inclined at an angle to the earth's surface in such a way that the cold air undercuts the warm air. Once again the balance maintained along the front between the two air masses is an extremely delicate one and is easily upset.

Depressions

A further complication will occur if the frontal zone forms beneath a divergent air stream in the upper westerlies. Air is now lifted to be incorporated in the jet stream resulting in a centre of low pressure at ground level. Not only does this cause air to spiral inwards in an anticlockwise direction in the northern hemisphere, it also causes a further disturbance to the front. A bulge or wave develops polewards so that the warmer, lighter air invades the colder, denser air to form a warm sector, and in this way a depression is formed. The leading edge of the warm sector becomes the warm front and the trailing edge the cold front and the whole system moves northeastwards with the Ferrel Westerlies (see figure 7.5).

At the same time as the warm air invades the cold air it also rises up the slope of the warm front. As it does so it increases in vorticity and curves cyclonically to be removed by the jet stream as shown in figure 7.6. Meanwhile to the rear of the depression, cold air descending from the convergence upstream of the trough in the upper westerlies loses spin and curves anticyclonically to become part of the circulation of the high pressure cell to the rear of the depression. In this way cold air in the upper westerlies is exchanged for warm air, so enabling the depression to fulfill part of its role as a means of heat exchange in the atmosphere. The process is illustrated again in figure 7.7 which shows a family of depressions with warm air rising in front of each one to join the jet stream and cold air descending in the rear to become part of the next anticyclone.

The weather in a depression

The weather produced by a depression depends on the behaviour of the air masses within it. First of all, because the coriolis force and the centrifugal force are both opposed to the pressure gradient force (see figure 7.3) the isobars are relatively close together. The gradient winds are therefore strong and they circle the centre of the depression in an anticlockwise direction in the northern hemisphere.

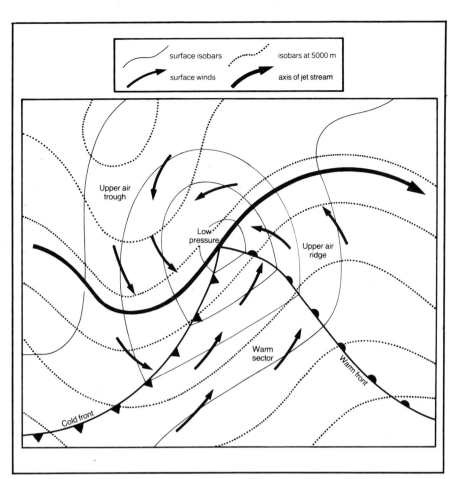

Fig 7.5   *A mature frontal depression in mid-latitudes and its relation to a trough in the upper westerlies*

Fig 7.6   *Diagram to show the exchange of upper air for surface air in a depression*

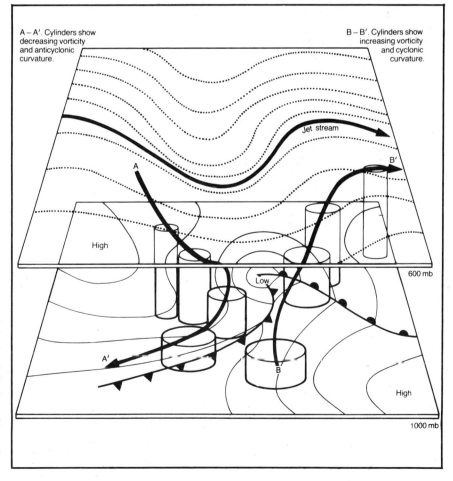

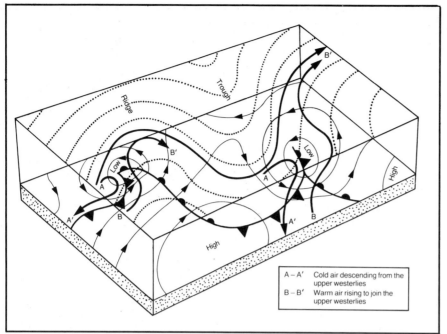

Fig 7.7   Diagram to show heat exchange between the upper and lower air in a family of mid-latitude frontal depressions

Fig 7.8   Map and section through a depression centred over the Irish Sea

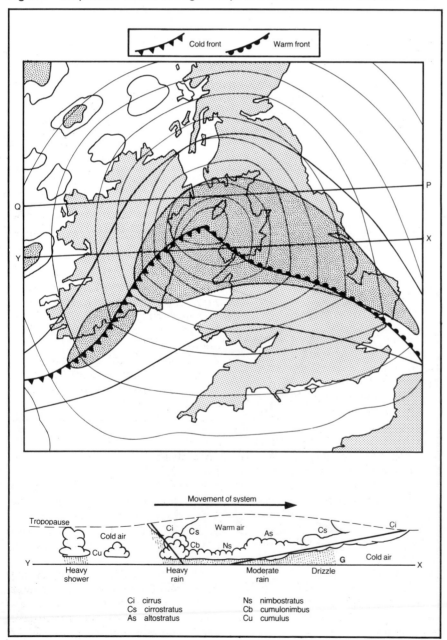

The development of a wave form between the cold and warm air masses traps the warm air between modified cold air in front and fresh cold air in the rear. As it is lighter the warm air tends to rise up the warm front and the cold front, but uplift is also encouraged by the behaviour of the fronts. The developing wave becomes more and more unstable as it grows in size, until by the time the wavelength is of the order of a few thousand kilometres, the whole system begins to decay. The wave now closes up, lifting the warm air clear of the ground as it does so. The result is adiabatic cooling on a vast scale producing great banks of cloud and extensive rainfall, especially along the fronts themselves.

The map in figure 7.8 shows a mature depression centred over the Irish Sea. Below it is a section along the line X – Y showing the location and attitude of the fronts, and the associated cloud. A person living in Grimsby, at the mouth of the Humber would be located at **G** on the section and the whole system would be moving towards him. High cirrus clouds, streaks of which so often herald the approach of a depression, already stretch out over the North Sea and the cloud base has been getting lower for an hour or so. The winds, obeying Buys Ballots Law, have been freshening from the southeast and it is already beginning to drizzle in Grimsby as altostratus cloud approaches.

For the next few hours the rain is likely to get heavier as the altostratus cloud is replaced by nimbostratus. The wind will continue to blow from the southeast and the temperature will remain cool. The passage of the warm front brings about more rapid change. The wind will veer to the southwest or west and strengthen and there will be quite a sudden rise in temperature of several degrees.

An hour or so later, hard on the heels of the warm front, the cold front will pass through. Its approach is heralded by towering cumulonimbus cloud and the onset of very heavy rain. Thunder and lightning are also likely, for the passage of a cold front is a frequent cause of thunderstorms in the British Isles. The temperature will fall again and the winds will suddenly veer to northwest and freshen considerably. In the past such a change would be a great danger to a sailing ship which still had too much canvas spread aloft and it was important for the master of the ship to be able to read the weather signs and so anticipate the approach of frontal weather even though, at that time, neither he nor anyone else knew that fronts existed!

As the depression moves eastwards the cloud will begin to break up giving sunny periods. The cold polar maritime air will bring with it very good visibility, but being warmed from below during its passage over the North Atlantic Drift it will also be highly unstable. Great towering banks of cumulus cloud will be carried along in the air stream, some of them producing short-lived but very heavy rain showers, and these too are often thundery.

Such a sequence of weather is typical of a mid-latitude frontal depression but it must be emphasised that no two depressions are ever exactly alike. For instance, the pattern of isobars is never the same in any two depressions and so the changes in the strength and direction of the winds is unique to any depression. Secondly, variations in the weather arise from the stage of development of the depression, as reference to figure 7.9 will quickly show. Even within one depression the weather sequence at any place depends on its location relative to the centre of the depression. Someone living in London will have a very different view of the weather generated by the depression in figure 7.8 than the person in Grimsby. Even today, one of the variables that bedevils forecasts is the exact line of travel taken by the depression. A change of only a few degrees over the Atlantic can move the belt of rain hundreds of miles to the north or south and so change the weather pattern over much of the country.

Finally, depressions can be divided into two broad types as shown in figure 7.10. In the first type, 'ana' fronts, the warm air is rising at all levels giving a very vigorous depression with prolonged and heavy precipitation. In contrast, 'kata' fronts occur when the difference in temperature between the warm air and the cold air in the depression is slight. In this situation the upper part of the troposphere is occupied by relatively dry subsiding air and so cloud development is limited in vertical extent and precipitation is slight. Kata fronts tend to be found in depressions travelling round the periphery of an anticyclone but it is also thought that ana fronts and kata fronts may be found in the same depression, with the former located nearer the centre.

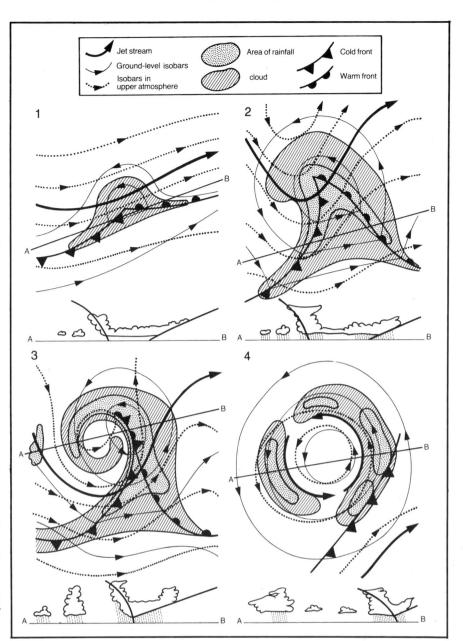

Fig 7.9   The life cycle of a depression

EXERCISES

7.1 Trace the fronts and the isobar pattern from the map in figure 7.8. Assuming the lowest isobar shown is 980 mb and the pressure interval to be 4 mb, number the isobars on your chart to show the distribution of pressure.

7.2 Using the correct symbols taken from figure 10.2 on page 55, draw on the chart in figure 7.8 the following station plots:
(i) At Liverpool: temp., 12°C; wind, SE force 4; sky overcast; weather, continuous very heavy rain.
(ii) At London: temp., 16°C; wind, SW force 2; sky half-covered with cloud; weather, light drizzle.
(iii) At Dublin: temp., 10°C; wind, NW force 7; sky three-quarters covered with cloud; weather, heavy showers and squalls.

7.3 Describe in detail the complete weather sequence experienced in Middlesborough if P – Q on figure 7.8 is the line of traverse through the depression.
7.4 Choose any other traverse through the depression and describe the weather sequence for further practice.

Frontolysis

Figure 7.9 shows the life-cycle of a depression in four stages. The first two diagrams illustrate frontogenesis or the birth of a depression described earlier in the chapter, while the second two illustrate the decay of a depression or frontolysis.

The air behind the cold front, curving down from the jet stream, has an anticyclonic curvature and so travels at a greater speed than the geostrophic wind. The subsiding wedge of cold air

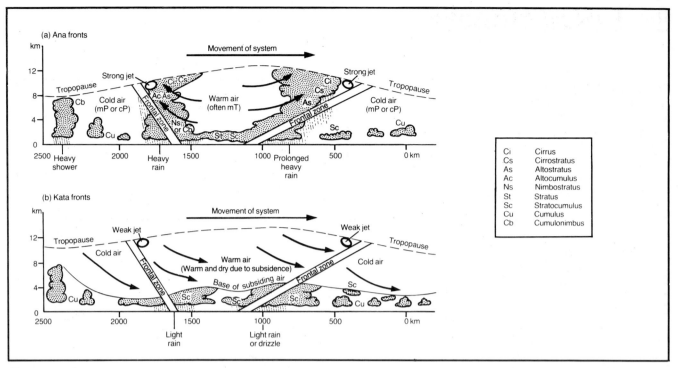

Fig 7.10   Sections through the two main kinds of depression

is therefore forced under the warm air so pushing it forward, also at a super-geostrophic speed. In so doing it acts like a scoop, forcing the warm air to rise rapidly up the cold front creating great instability (2).

In contrast the warm front of the depression tends to move at the same speed as the air in the warm sector. As a result the cold front travels more quickly than the warm front, and begins to overtake it, starting at the tip of the warm sector and working outwards. When this process occurs the air in the warm sector is pinched out and lifted bodily off the ground (3). The resulting adiabatic cooling promotes the condensation of the water vapour content, so producing the clouds and rain. Eventually all that remains of the once vigorous depression is a roughly circular anticlockwise swirl of air in the upper troposphere, often referred to as a cut-off low (4).

Once the warm air has finally been lifted off the ground the cold air behind the depression comes into contact with the cold air in front. It is unlikely that the two air masses will be exactly the same and so the zone of separation between the two is referred to as an occlusion or occluded front.

If the air behind the warm sector is colder than the air in front then the occlusion is known as a cold occlusion, while if the reverse is true it is called a warm occlusion. Both possibilities are shown in figure 7.11.

Although adiabatic cooling occurs in the warm air as it is lifted off the ground, the resulting condensation of water vapour in the rising air mass releases a great deal of latent heat, so

that when it eventually becomes part of the upper westerlies it is a great deal warmer than it would otherwise have been. The vapour condensed was gained by the air mass as it lay over its source region, perhaps in the tropical North Atlantic. In this way solar energy from the tropics is stored in the air mass and carried polewards to be

released when condensation eventually occurs, so completing the process of heat exchange in the atmosphere in which the mid-latitude frontal depression plays such a crucial role.

Fig 7.11   Occlusions in a frontal depression

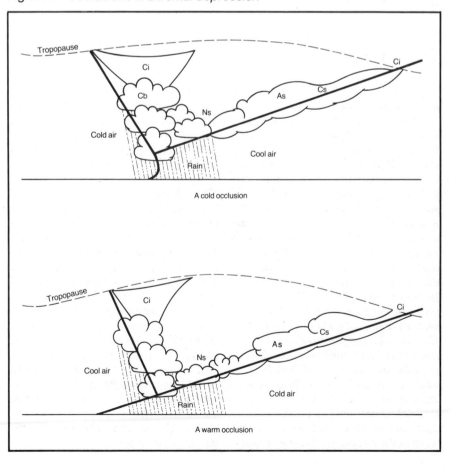

44

8 Local climate

For an individual person nothing can be more local than the climate to which he is being subjected and so it seems appropriate to look briefly at the physiological effects of climate.

The human body functions at the very specific temperature of 37°C and only a small variation either side of this will indicate that something is wrong. This temperature is maintained by a balance between the generation of heat within the body and the loss of heat from skin and lungs. If the climate is such that this balance is difficult to maintain then the result is physical discomfort.

The sensation of warmth or chill experienced by the body depends on three factors: the temperature of the surrounding air; the rate of evaporation of moisture from skin and lungs; and ventilation by moving air. As figure 8.1 shows, as long as there are no extremes of humidity the body is comfortable at temperatures between 20°C and 27°C. Below 20°C irritation sets in unless activity is possible, and warmer clothing is necessary to cut down loss of heat. As the temperature of the environment falls, better insulation is required or heating systems must be used to create an artificial environment. Generally speaking 'dry cold' is more endurable than 'wet cold' for if the skin is damp the slightest breeze will increase heat loss through evaporation. It is true to say that high winds are the greatest enemy of the traveller in polar regions.

Temperatures in excess of 27°C also cause discomfort unless a way of losing heat can be found. Our usual solution is to wear less clothing, to go bathing or take a shower. Again water will cool us off and as our skin dries we lose body heat to effect the necessary evaporation. If the air is very dry, however, the relief is short-lived and if we are to avoid sunstroke we will need to get into the shade.

As with low temperatures, heat is harder to bear in the presence of humidity. As explained in chapter 5 this is because excess body heat is lost by perspiration, but in a humid atmosphere the perspiration cannot easily be evaporated unless there is a breeze. One way of making it possible to work indoors in hot climates is therefore to provide electric fans, although these days air conditioning is used increasingly to lower the air temperature. In tropical cities ugly air conditioning units can be seen fixed to the outside walls of the buildings, and it is common

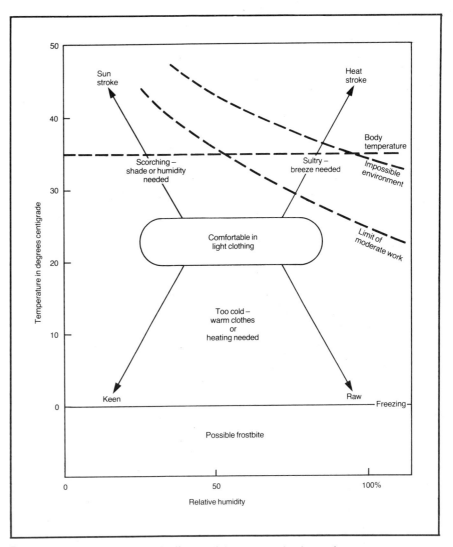

Fig 8.1   The physiological effects of the atmospheric environment

to find that possession of air conditioning is a sign of status. In some cases it may be so much cooler inside an office that it may actually feel uncomfortable to someone who has just walked in from outside, and it is noticeable that banks are frequent offenders in this respect!

The influence of latitude

Since the heating effect of sunlight depends a great deal on the angle at which it strikes the ground (see chapter 4) latitude is an important determinant in local climate. Figure 8.2 shows the path of the sun across the sky at a number of selected latitudes in the northern hemisphere. The diagrams clearly show how in the tropics the sun rises almost vertically from the horizon so that dawn and dusk are short-lived. At the same time the sun remains high in the sky for a large part of the day which is of much the same duration throughout the year, so leaving little scope for seasonal variation in the pattern of weather.

At the tropic of cancer the pattern begins to change and while the sun is overhead at midday in June it remains well away from the zenith during December. Also there begins to be a noticeable difference between the length of day in June compared to that in December. This difference becomes increasingly marked with distance from the equator in mid-latitudes until at the arctic circle the sun only just touches the horizon at midday in December and again at midnight in June. The mid-summer path of the sun at the arctic circle also shows the long, slow rise and fall of the sun, morning and evening, when the shadows are long (figure 8.3). Even at midday in these high latitudes the elevation of the sun is never great. Finally at the north pole we see how the sun journeys around the horizon at the equinoxes and stays at an elevation of 23½° for the whole 24 hours at the summer solstice.

Figure 8.4 shows the path of the sun across the sky during the equinoxes

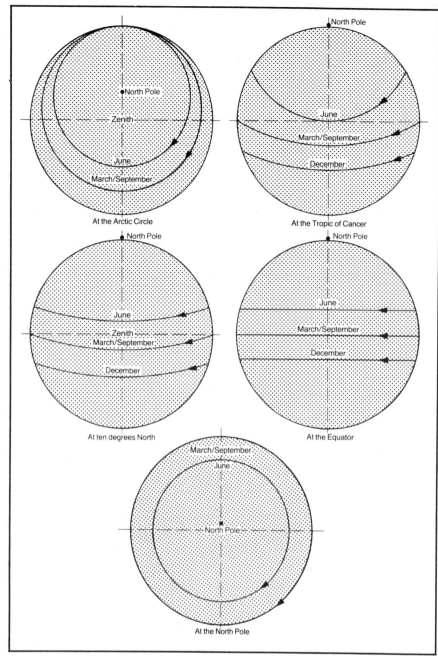

Fig 8.2   The sun's path for various latitudes in the northern hemisphere

and the solstices for the London area at latitude 51°N and on the Greenwich Meridian; it illustrates the changing length of day through the year and the changing angle of the midday sun experienced in these latitudes. However, the passage of the sun across the sky also affects the amount of shade provided by buildings and vegetation. During June, although there are certainly long shadows morning and evening, for much of the day the sun is high in the sky and shadows are not important in the local climate. In mid-winter, however, the angle of incidence of sunlight is always small and even at midday many places will remain in shade. The variation in temperature between places in shade and places in direct sunlight can be most marked and can have an important effect on the location of different plants.

Vegetation itself is of course an influence on temperature variations within the local area. Different kinds of vegetation produce different degrees of shade and reflect different amounts of solar radiation. Forests are believed to reflect 9 to 18 per cent depending on the type of tree, grassland around 25 per cent, desert sand up to 30 or 40 per cent and fresh snow 85 or even 90 per cent. Again the values for the albedo of any surface vary with the angle of incidence of the sun's rays and therefore with latitude and the season of the year. For example, a calm water surface will reflect only 2 to 3 per cent for angles exceeding 60° but more than 50 per cent at an angle of only 15°.

Local relief

Local relief is important in local climate because it may alter significantly the angle of incidence of solar radiation. North-facing slopes serve to reduce the angle of incidence while south-facing slopes serve to increase it. This factor is referred to as aspect. As most landscapes can be regarded as an assemblage of slopes this can give rise to significant local variation in temperature; the greater the relief the greater this variation will be.

It is especially important in the local climates of high latitudes where there is a far greater seasonal variation in the angle of incidence of sunlight. Thus in winter, steep slopes which face south are able to compensate almost completely for the low sun and tend to be the warmest, while in summer when the sun is much higher in the sky, the more gentle south-facing slopes benefit most. On the other hand north-facing

Fig 8.3   Long shadows around midday in high latitudes

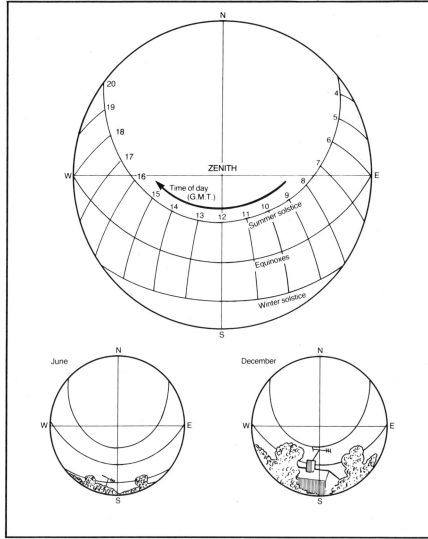

Fig 8.4   Sun path model for the London area, showing the shading of a suburban garden in June and December at midday

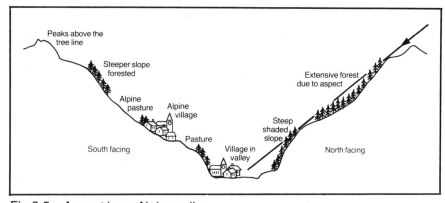

Fig 8.5   Aspect in an Alpine valley

slopes may rarely see the sun at all except on clear days in mid-summer (see figure 8.5).

The grain of the country may also be a factor, as valleys which run from west to east will result in a large proportion of slopes that face either north or south and which therefore concentrate or disperse solar radiation over the ground. Furthermore, in high latitudes where sunrise and sunset are prolonged, east and southeast slopes get morning light while west and southwest slopes get afternoon and evening light. Since morning air is frequently clearer with less cloud cover, east and southeast facing slopes tend to record more hours of sunshine and are often favoured by plant communities containing some different species from those that face west or southwest.

A further influence on local climate for which slopes are responsible is shelter, especially where there is a prevailing wind direction. In the British Isles east-facing slopes are usually protected but it must be remembered that they are also exposed to the occasional biting east wind which may be far more significant for wild plants and for crops. Snow in particular may lie far longer on these slopes and it is noticeable that in our glaciated uplands, corrie glaciation has bitten far more deeply into the landscape on east and northeast-facing slopes which are sheltered from the mild westerly winds.

Lowland basins that are surrounded by hills on all sides benefit from shelter, and diffuse sky radiation becomes more effective in sharing out heat energy among slopes with differing aspects. In the British Isles, lowland basins are also warmer in summer and for that reason local thunderstorms are particularly prevalent in such areas. Alternatively, as described in chapter 5, during long winter nights valleys and hollows in the landscape form reservoirs of cold air that drains off the surrounding hills, and the significantly increased incidence of frost is a very important factor in the location of crops which are liable to frost damage.

Mountain climates

If local relief affects the climate in lowland areas then the effect is far greater in mountain areas where every difference in degree of slope with respect to the sun's rays, produces a different micro-climate. The result is that highland climates are mosaics of innumerable micro-climates that correspond to the intricate pattern of relief and altitude.

Due to their altitude, mountain areas have lower air temperatures than nearby lowland areas, and in general temperature falls at around 6.5°C per 1000 m. Also, as a result of the lower air pressure at high altitudes, air temperature decreases rapidly from the ground upwards. Not only are temperatures low in high mountains but because of the rapid changes in the height of the ground surface there must be great temperature variation within relatively small areas.

Although temperatures in mountains are low, solar radiation makes a vital contribution to the unique character of mountain climates. Low temperatures result in a low absolute humidity (see *Humidity* on page 16), and the low air pressure together with lack of dust particles allows a much higher proportion of short wave, ultra-violet radiation to reach the ground. At the same time, where there is snow there is also a great deal of reflected light, so that while the

Fig 8.6   View in the Swiss Alps showing north and south facing slopes

Fig 8.7   Skiers in sunny Austrian weather

slopes to a greater intensity of insolation causes the air to expand and rise, and there is a flow of air up the slopes from the valley bottoms. Again air will flow along the valleys from lower ones into higher ones to create an anabatic wind. In this way the relief may be the greatest influence on the strength and direction of the winds in the mountains which can be quite at variance with that aloft or over adjacent lowlands.

In some cases the configuration of mountain valleys may combine to produce regional mountain winds of some significance. Such winds are the Mistral of southern France, the Bora of the Adriatic coast and the Santa Ana of southern California. The Mistral in particular is a current of cold air which flows down the mountain valleys and down the Rhône valley towards the Mediterranean, but it is often intensified by the passage of a depression along the Mediterranean Sea. The threat this wind poses to crops sensitive to frost damage is so serious that thick evergreen hedges have been planted across the valley to break the force of the wind and to provide as much protection as possible.

Although winds in mountainous country are often funnelled by the terrain there are other effects that are significant in the local climate. Although friction with the surface of the earth is high owing to the rugged countryside, the higher slopes may well be above the level where surface friction is really effective. Wind speeds are therefore generally high and winds are often very gusty because of the high relief. Coupled with the low air temperatures this is a major problem for climbers operating at great altitude and they are very vulnerable to exposure.

A good example of the barrier effect of high mountain ranges, mentioned previously, is the Pacific Northwest of America which is protected from the cold air mass over the continental interior by the Rockies. Another good example is the mild Chinook which frees the high plains from snow in spring; it is described in chapter 5.

Fogginess is usually greater in mountains than in the nearby lowlands, but although radiation fog is quite common on clear nights, a great deal of mountain fog is simply low cloud. For this reason precipitation is universally greater in uplands for as air is lifted over higher ground adiabatic cooling must occur resulting in cloud and heavy precipitation, especially on windward slopes. In high winds a good deal of

sun is out it is possible to feel quite comfortable in light clothing and the low air temperature is merely refreshing and invigorating. Indeed, sunburn is also a very real danger. As soon as the sun goes behind the clouds or a nearby peak, however, it will turn very chilly. If it is either sunny or dull it is possible to dress accordingly but with scattered and patchy clouds rapid temperature change is quite a problem; variations of the order of 10°C can occur within a few seconds (figure 8.7).

R. Geiger in *The Climate near the Ground* quotes temperatures of 80°C on southwest-facing slopes in the high mountains of Otztal in Austria on a July day and only 23°C on a northeast-facing slope in the same area. Shade is an additional factor on steep mountain slopes adding to the contrasts resulting from aspect. So vital is it in the local climate of the European Alps that in east-west valleys a major distinction can be made between the north-facing and south-facing sides (see figures 8.5 and 6). Very steep slopes are normally forested anyway but the gentler upper slopes on the north side of the valley are

used as alpine pastures. The south side is far more extensively forested. There are also many more villages on the north side of the valley than on the south side and it has even been claimed that people in villages that get the benefit of the sun are on average more intelligent. Whether or not that is true there is sufficient difference in the local climate for the two sides of the valleys to be given different names: *Sonnenseite* and *Schattenseite* in German and in French *l'adret* and *l'ubac*.

A further factor in temperature variations in the mountains is the effect of night-time radiation which because of the thin, clear air is particularly effective on calm, cloudless nights. A distinctive feature of mountain climates is the large diurnal range of temperature. Cold air is of course rather heavy and a further consequence is that air tends to drain down the slopes and into the valleys at night. It will also flow along the valley bottoms and so pass from higher valleys into lower ones. Such a wind is known as a katabatic wind. In the daytime the reverse occurs. The exposure of the higher mountain

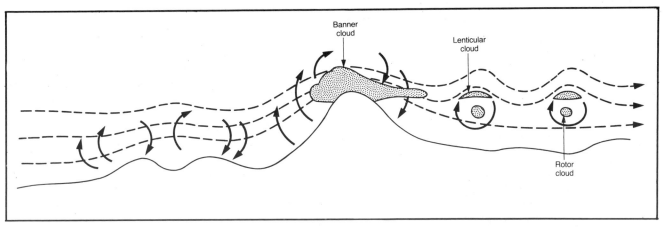

Fig 8.8 Clouds due to turbulence over mountain barriers

turbulence is caused by the mountain ridges below and generally speaking updraughts occur on the windward side and downdraughts on the leeward side (see figure 8.8). Higher peaks are frequently capped by a 'banner cloud' which is drawn out into a long tail by the strong air flow, while further downstream standing waves occur with lenticular clouds forming in the crests and rotor clouds below, both resulting from the overturning of the air.

Coasts

It can be very frustrating to set off for a day's fishing or sailing only to find on arrival at the coast that the water is too rough for it to be safe to put to sea. The high waves may be the result of a swell reaching the shore from a storm far out to sea, but they may also occur simply because the wind is quite a lot stronger than inland because there is less shelter.

Weather on the coast is frequently different from that a few miles inland and it is not safe to assume that because it is warm and sunny at home it will be the same by the sea. During the summer the sea is cooler than the land and mist may form over the sea and drift in over the coast. Such a sea fret can be persistent and even on a clear day it may take some time for the sun to lift the mist and break through. Some coasts suffer particularly from this phenomenon especially where ocean currents pull away from the land encouraging cold water to well up from the depths just off shore. Peru and California demonstrate this particularly well. The cold water surface cools the lower layers of the atmosphere and sets up an inversion so that the sea fog becomes trapped along with smoke and exhaust fumes. As there are more cars per family in California than anywhere else in the world this is a particular problem here and temperatures along the coast are markedly lower than inland.

The temperature difference between land and sea can also affect the amount of sunshine a place enjoys. In Britain, duration of sunshine is greatest in the south and highest of all in a strip along the south coast, with Eastbourne and Worthing each claiming an average of just over five hours per day. This is mainly because, in summer, as the day progresses the land becomes increasingly warmer than the sea and local convection currents develop. Soon banks of cumulus cloud begin to build in the sky inland, but over the sea there is far less activity and it frequently remains relatively clear.

The temperature difference that exists between land and sea is also responsible for local winds known as land and sea breezes. At night the land cools relatively rapidly, especially with clear skies, while over the sea the air holds its temperature due to the warmth available in the water. Air warmed by contact with the water surface will begin to rise and be replaced by cool, heavy air flowing off the land. So effective is this air flow that it is possible to smell the vegetation well out to sea and before the land is sighted. During the day the reverse occurs. Local heating over the land causes strong thermals to develop and cool air from over the sea moves inland to form a sea breeze. Sadly for the holidaymaker, longer hours of sunshine are too often offset by sea breezes and so windbreaks have become standard equipment on British beaches.

Urban climates

Until the eighteenth century, when the foundations of the Industrial Revolution were laid in Britain, there were few cities and they were still relatively small by modern standards. Since then, however, an ever increasing proportion of the human race has come to live in large cities and in the United Kingdom over 80 per cent of the population live in cities of over 100,000 people. Since 1950 the proportion has begun to fall again but only very slowly. Elsewhere, especially in the Developing World, urbanisation is continuing at a staggering rate. By the year 2000 AD the United Nations calculate that worldwide, the number of people living in an urban environment will exceed those living in a rural one for the first time in history.

The concentration of human activity in cities, and especially man's increasing consumption of energy for heating, air conditioning, transport and industrial processes, has served to modify the local climate quite considerably. One important effect is to create heat islands, and figure 8.9 illustrates the point by showing the temperature distribution in San Francisco on a spring evening and the minimum temperatures for London on a May night. The effect tends to be more marked at night when the release of heat into the air is not masked by incoming solar radiation; however, even on clear summer days the production of heat energy in heavily industrialised areas can amount to as much as 10 per cent of that received by insolation.

British cities may be as much as 8°C warmer than surrounding rural areas on a winter's night, and clearly the combustion of fossil fuels is a significant factor, but it is by no means the only one. A great variety of solids, liquids and gases are poured into the atmosphere over a city, the most important pollutants being smoke particles, sulphur dioxide and carbon dioxide. Although the higher concentration of dust seems to scatter a larger proportion of solar radiation at the ultra-violet end of the spectrum back into space, it also enables the air to absorb more of the heat radiated back by the city below. This is a factor of considerable importance for the materials of which a city is constructed, brick, stone, concrete and asphalt, all have a higher heat capacity than soil or vegetation. Heat stored in the mass of buildings and roads is gradually released, so delaying the nightly fall in temperature compared with the surrounding countryside. The onset of winter is also tempered by heat released from the fabric of a city so that seasonal changes of temperature also lag behind those in the countryside and

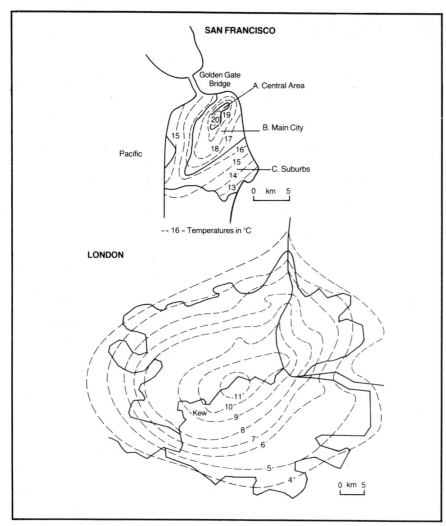

San Francisco

SAN FRANCISCO

Golden Gate Bridge

A. Central Area

19
20
19

B. Main City

15
17
18   16
15
14   C. Suburbs
13

Pacific

0   km   5

-- 16 - Temperatures in °C

LONDON

11
10
Kew   9
8
7
6
5
4

0   km   5

Fig 8.9   Heat islands

so help to produce temperature differences. Finally, towns are better drained than rural areas. Surface water rapidly disappears underground and snow is cleared from the roads and paths. In this way less solar energy is required for the melting of snow and the evaporation of water and so more is available to heat the air.

The dust produced by the combustion of fossil fuels has a further effect on the local climate of urban areas. Smoke particles provide nuclei for the condensation of water vapour and so encourage the formation of fog, while the lower temperatures that cause the condensation in the first place also lead to increased consumption of fuel for heating purposes so that the two tendencies reinforce each other. Fogs of this kind, containing a high concentration of atmospheric pollution are known as smogs and were particularly bad in London in the early 1950s, when thousands died from respiratory conditions aggravated by the polluted air. Since then the Clean Air Act of 1956 has successfully reduced the level of atmospheric pollution in British cities and fogs are less dense and occur less frequently.

The storing of heat in brick and concrete not only affects city temperatures but has also been shown to trigger summer thunderstorms, and London has a higher susceptibility to thunderstorm rain than the surrounding region. The rainfall may even be heavier as a result of the more vigorous convection and the larger number of condensation nuclei present in the atmosphere. However, the lack of plants in an urban area and the rapid removal of surface water in drains and sewers means that the air in a large town may well have a lower relative humidity than in the surrounding countryside. Increased cloudiness over cities and the prevalence of fogs also tend to reduce the hours of sunshine enjoyed by city dwellers.

Most of the effects described above are more noticeable under calm conditions. When there is an appreciable wind the dust and fumes, as well as the warmer air, tend to be blown downwind of the city and if wind speeds exceed 5 m per second they are likely to be dispersed altogether. As in mountains the 'roughness' produced by the presence of so many buildings can create considerable turbulence in the air when the winds are strong. Among high rise flats or the downtown skyscrapers of American cities, streets can be turned into narrow canyons that funnel and concentrate the effects of the wind. Some streets, and especially those in cities outside the tropics, which are aligned east-west may be almost permanently in shade, so adding yet another dimension to urban climates.

Global effects

Before the Industrial Revolution the majority of people lived by farming and the pattern of people's lives was largely determined by the slow progression of the seasons. Today, far from being at the mercy of his environment, man is increasingly able to adapt it to suit his needs as a result of his rapidly developing technology. Unfortunately, while increasing urbanisation, industrialisation and deforestation on a worldwide scale may seem to offer continued improvements in living standards, scientists are increasingly concerned about the changes that are occurring in the atmosphere as a result. Everywhere the ice sheets are on the retreat since the last glacial maximum around 1750 and mean surface temperatures seem to have risen about 1°C over the last hundred years.

The reason for this global warming would appear to be the increasing concentrations of carbon dioxide in the atmosphere. It is estimated that we release around 8×10^9 tonnes of carbon dioxide into the atmosphere every year. Three-quarters of this total results from the burning of fossil fuels and the remaining one quarter through farming. It is estimated that the oceans exchange something like 100×10^9 tonnes of carbon dioxide with the atmosphere annually while living organisms cycle a further 60×10^9 tonnes. As most of the latter is attributable to the world's forests which are rapidly being cleared the build up of carbon dioxide in the atmosphere is likely to continue unless the oceans can absorb more. Estimates suggest that the concentration of carbon dioxide in the atmosphere has increased by 35 parts per million over the last hundred years to reach the present figure of 315 parts per million and that 350 parts per million may be possible by 2000 AD.

The danger is that nobody can be certain what the effects of this global warming are likely to be. Meanwhile, as the world population grows and man makes increasing demands on the environment, the possibility exists that the natural balance may be upset with possibly disastrous results.

9 Recording the weather

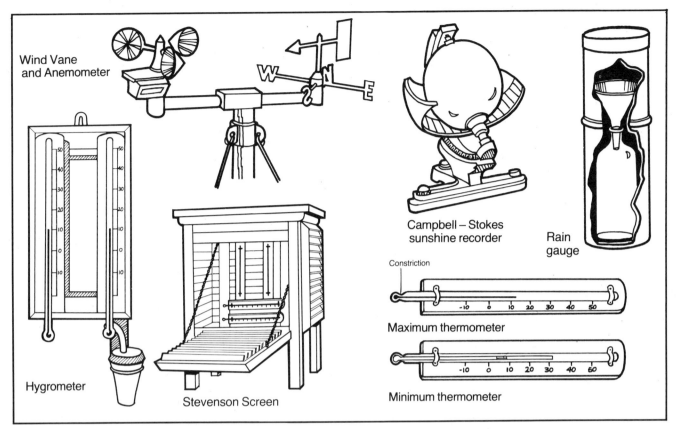

Fig 9.1   Weather recording instruments

As with any science, our progress in understanding atmospheric processes depends to a great extent on the availability of accurate measurements and it is a measure of the economic and strategic value of good weather forecasts that so much expensive hardware is at present deployed to provide the forecasters with the data they need. Weather records are necessarily made at selected locations on the earth's surface and conditions between these weather stations must therefore be inferred. It follows that the closer the network of recording stations the more detailed and accurate the forecasts can be.

The simple weather station

A basic understanding of weather recording can be obtained by looking at a simple weather station. The typical school weather station may contain anything up to eight or nine instruments, which can measure temperature, humidity, pressure, the speed and direction of the wind, rainfall and insolation.

As far as possible the instruments should be reposed under standard conditions so that recordings made at different stations are comparable. This is particularly true of thermometers which must always record the shade temperature. For this reason they are housed in an enclosure known as a Stevenson Screen, which is shown in figure 9.1. This is simply a box painted white to reflect insolation. It has louvred sides which allow a free flow of air to reach the instruments inside but at the same time protect them from direct sunlight. It should stand 112 cm above the ground and well away from trees and buildings that might influence the temperatures recorded.

Most weather stations measure the maximum and minimum temperatures for each twenty four hours. The minimum thermometer is an alcohol thermometer with a pin contained in the column of alcohol. Due to surface tension there is a 'skin effect' at the end of the column furthest from the bulb forming a meniscus. As the temperature falls the alcohol in the bulb contracts so that the column of alcohol is withdrawn down the tube. As a result the meniscus catches the pin and pulls it back towards the bulb. Once the temperature begins to rise again the pin is left stranded in the tube registering the minimum temperature.

The maximum thermometer is a mercury thermometer with a constriction in the tube just above the bulb. As the temperature rises the mercury in the bulb expands driving a thread of mercury through the constriction and up the tube. When the temperature begins to fall again the mercury thread is trapped in the tube so recording the maximum temperature. A mercury thermometer without a constriction can be used to give the actual temperature at any given time.

A fourth instrument that depends on temperature for its operation is the wet and dry bulb thermometer or hygrometer. This measures humidity and depends on the principles of evaporation for its operation. Two identical thermometers are placed side by side, but the bulb of one is kept damp by being wrapped in a muslin bag, the end of which is immersed in a reservoir of water. Moisture is continually lost from the bag by evaporation and the rate depends on the humidity of the air. The heat responsible for the evaporation is drawn from the bulb of the thermometer resulting in a depression of the wet bulb temperature. The difference between the wet bulb and dry bulb temperatures is therefore a measure of the humidity. The values of the absolute humidity, the relative humidity and the dewpoint temperature can be obtained from a set of hygrometric tables.

Although the mercury barometer, invented by Torricelli in 1643, is a simple and accurate instrument it is large and not very portable. For this reason an aneroid barometer is more frequently used. The heart of the instrument is a thin walled metal box from which the air has been evacuated. Increases in air pressure force the walls of the box inwards while falling air pressure allows the walls to recover. These movements are magnified by a system of levers which finally operate a pointer which moves over a graduated scale. More valuable still is a barograph in which the levers operate a pen which produces a continuous record of pressure changes on a revolving drum.

As wind speed and direction are affected by friction with the ground, measurements are taken at an international standard height of 10 m. The direction is given by a wind vane located well away from disturbing influences such as buildings or trees. The vane consists of a vertical, flat surface and the action of the wind pushing against it moves the pointer in the direction from which the wind is blowing. Wind speed can be estimated using the scale devised by Admiral Sir Francis Beaufort in 1805 and shown in figure 9.2. More accurate, however, is the cup anemometer. This consists of three cups mounted on a spindle, which in turn is connected to a rev-counter. The wind blows against the cups causing the spindle to rotate, and the number of revolutions recorded in a given time gives the wind speed.

The rain gauge has an accurately turned brass rim 12.7 cm in diameter. Rain falling inside the rim is funnelled into a collecting jar held inside a copper can. To prevent the evaporation of the water which has been collected, the copper can hangs inside an outer copper

cylinder to which a funnel is attached, thus creating an insulating jacket of air. When a reading is taken the water in the jar is poured into a measuring cylinder graduated for the rain gauge.

Cloud cover is estimated by eye, and is measured in eighths or oktas, while the form and height of the cloud is also assessed by reference to its appearance. Duration of sunshine, however, can be accurately recorded by a Campbell-Stokes sunshine recorder. This consists of a glass sphere which acts as a lens, focussing the sunlight on to a sensitised card. Whenever the sun shines a brown line is scorched on to the blue card so recording its duration.

EXERCISES

9.1 Imagine you have been given the money to set up a weather station.
(i) List the instruments you would buy and explain your choice.
(ii) Investigate your local area to find the best location for the station and say what its advantages are.
(iii) Describe how you would place and expose each of the instruments you have chosen.

Professional weather forecasting
The instruments used by the Meteorological Office in their weather stations are not very different from those in a school weather station but they are of course more accurate and may give more detailed information. Thus the Stevenson Screen will contain a maximum and a minimum thermometer and a wet and dry bulb thermo-

meter, but a continuous record of temperature and humidity is also kept by means of a thermograph and a hygrograph. The rain gauge is also rather more sophisticated and not only records the amount of rain but also the rate at which it falls over a twenty-four hour period.

The locations of the land-based weather stations of the Meteorological Office are shown on figure 9.3 as well as the location of the four ocean weather ships which supply vital information about the weather over the Atlantic to the west of the British Isles. This is supplemented by weather information from ships of the Merchant Navy which make observations on a voluntary basis during their journeys around the world, and from the coastguard service. At the same time automatic weather stations help to fill in the remaining gaps in remote areas such as the Shetland Islands or on North Sea gas and oil platforms. In this way a fairly complete picture of the weather around the British Isles is constantly available.

The influence of conditions in the upper atmosphere has already been stressed and soundings are taken daily using radio-sondes which consist of a package of instruments carried aloft by a balloon. These may reach as high as 30 km or more before the balloon bursts and the instrument package returns to earth by parachute. The sonde is tracked by radar to give wind speed and direction while a transmitter continuously reports the details of temperature, humidity and pressure to ground-based computers.

Over the last twenty years satellites have added a further dimension to

Fig 9.2   The Beaufort scale of wind speed

	The Beaufort Scale		
Beaufort Number	Description of the wind	Speed of the wind in knots	Possible effects of the wind
0	Calm	Less than 1	Smoke rises vertically
1	Light air	1–3	Direction of the wind is shown by smoke drift but not by the wind vane
2	Light breeze	4–6	Wind felt on the face; leaves rustle; wind vanes are moved by the wind
3	Gentle breeze	7–10	Leaves and twigs are in constant motion; the wind extends a light flag
4	Moderate breeze	11–16	Dust and loose paper are raised; the small branches of trees are moved
5	Fresh breeze	17–21	Small trees begin to sway; crested wavelets form on inland water
6	Strong breeze	22–27	Large branches of trees begin to move; telegraph wires whistle; umbrellas are difficult to use
7	Moderate gale	28–33	Whole trees are set in motion; some difficulty in walking against the wind
8	Fresh gale	34–40	Twigs break off trees; great difficulty in walking against the wind
9	Strong gale	41–47	Slight structural damage is caused; chimney pots and slates are removed
10	Whole gale	48–55	Trees are uprooted; much damage to buildings is caused. This wind is seldom experienced inland
11	Storm	56–63	Widespread damage occurs. This wind is rarely experienced in Britain
12	Hurricane	More than 64	The whole countryside is devastated

weather observation. Geostationary satellites maintain a constant position some 36,000 km above the earth and continuously scan one large area of the earth's surface. Photographs produced every thirty minutes record the movement and development of weather systems within the scanned area.

Polar orbiting satellites circle the earth every two hours or so at a height between 700 km and 1,500 km. As their paths go from pole to pole, each successive pass over the equator is about 30° west of the previous one as the earth rotates beneath it. Again pictures of cloud patterns reveal the constantly changing weather conditions as well as the extent of snow cover and sea ice.

It is readily apparent that weather information quickly becomes out of date and so rapid communications between the members of the World Meteorological Organisation are vital. For this reason a global telecommunication system has been established with the primary centres in Washington, Moscow and Melbourne. The telecommunications centre at Bracknell is responsible for the collection, processing, distribution and exchange of weather data with the minimum of delay, and a complex of computers and teleprinters is available to make this possible. Indeed it is the modern computer that allows the meteorologist to process the enormous volume of data sufficiently quickly to prevent it becoming out of date before it can be used. In this way the forecaster can call on a great volume of incoming information in making his predictions.

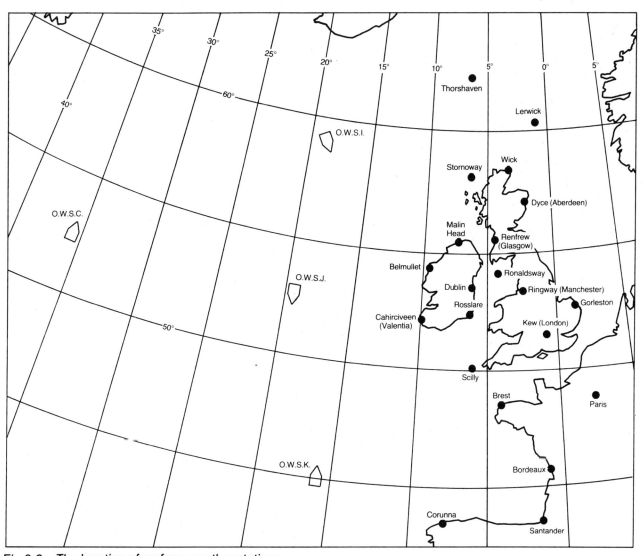

Fig 9.3   The location of surface weather stations

To enable the meteorologist to handle the large volume of data, observations from weather stations are transmitted in code and then translated into symbols which can be plotted on a map. Figure 10.1 shows a block of observations for 06 hours on 14 August 1979. At that time the Fastnet Race was in progress and a large number of sailing vessels were in the Celtic Sea south of Ireland. The readings for Scilly (code 804 in the left-hand column) were produced by a deep depression centred over Dublin moving eastwards over the British Isles.

Plotting the data

In order to plot the data on to the chart a station model is used. Each weather station is located on the map by means of a circle. This is illustrated by figure 10.1 which shows the standard plotting scheme and the station plot for Scilly at 06 hours. The symbols that are used are shown in figure 10.2.

Cloud amount (N) is measured in eighths or oktas on a scale from 0 to 8 and for increasing cloud cover more and more of the station circle is shaded as shown in the key. If the sky is obscured by fog then a diagonal cross is placed in the circle. The first figure in the code denotes cloud cover and so Scilly has three oktas at 06 hours.

Wind direction (dd) and wind speed (ff) are plotted by means of an arrow, the point of which is embedded in the station circle. The shaft of the arrow is drawn so that it approaches the station circle in the direction from which the wind is blowing. The second and third figures in the code give the bearing in tens of degrees, in this case 26 and so a bearing of 260°, which is very nearly due west. Figures four and five in the first block of the code give the wind speed in knots. This is portrayed on the chart by adding feathers to the arrow, each half-feather representing five knots and each full feather ten knots. A total calm is denoted by a second circle and a light wind of only one or two knots by an arrow without feathers. Wind speeds in excess of two knots are then plotted to the nearest five knots. Thus for Scilly 31 knots is shown on the station plot by three full feathers.

The second block of figures in the code gives visibility (VV), present weather (ww) and past weather (W). Reference to the meteorological office code (obtainable from Her Majesty's Stationary Office) will show that 65 represents a visibility of 15 kms, 25 means showers of rain currently in the area and 8 that past weather also con-

sisted of showers which followed along behind the cold front.

Barometric pressure (PPP) and air temperature (TT) are shown in the third block of figures. Pressure reduced to mean sea level is shown in millibars and tenths of millibars and only the last three figures are given so that 134 will represent a pressure of 1013.4 mb and 906 a pressure of 990.6 mb. This is simply because pressure at sea level is normally within the range 950 mb to 1050 mb and so it is comparatively easy to decide whether to add the digit 9 or the digits 1 and 0 in front of the given figures. The figures 983 therefore show that Scilly had a barometric pressure of 998.3 mb at 06 hours. Air temperature is more straightforward and is shown to the nearest whole degree celsius so that Scilly had a temperature of 14°C.

The next block of the code is concerned with clouds. The first figure gives the amount of cloud cover for the lowest cloud present (Nh). The second figure gives the form of the low level cloud (O_L) and the third the height above the ground of the lowest cloud. The last two figures in the code give the form of the medium level clouds (C_M) and the high level clouds (C_H). The symbols used are shown in figure 10.2 and the code shows that Scilly had 3 oktas of cumulus and strato-cumulus cloud with a cloud base between 300 and 600 m. No other clouds were present.

Of the remaining figures in the code only the barometric tendency (pp) is shown on the station plot. For Scilly it was 07 which means that over the previous three hours the pressure had

Fig 10.1   *The standard plotting scheme and the observations for Scilly at 06 hours on Tuesday 14 August 1979*

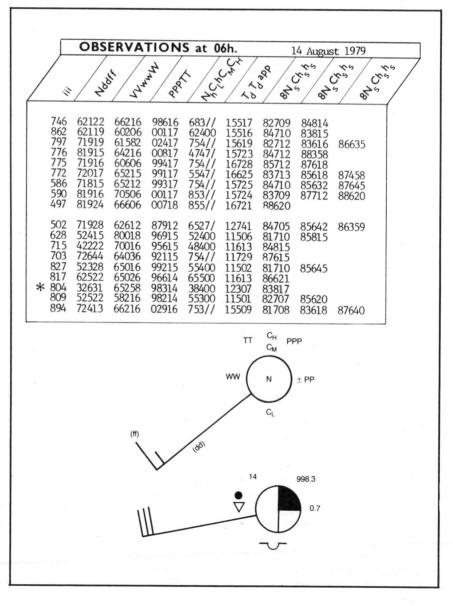

iii	Nddff	VVwwW	PPPTT	$N_hC_LhC_H$ C_M	T_dT_d aPP	$8NC_Hh_s$ C_Ls	$8NC_Hh_s$ C_Ls	$8NC_Hh_s$ C_Ls
746	62122	66216	98616	683//	15517	82709	84814	
862	62119	60206	00117	62400	15516	84710	83815	
797	71919	61582	02417	754//	15619	82712	83616	86635
776	81915	64216	00817	4747/	15723	84712	88358	
775	71916	60606	99417	754//	16728	85712	87618	
772	72017	65215	99117	5547/	16625	83713	85618	87458
586	71815	65212	99317	754//	15725	84710	85632	87645
590	81916	70506	00117	853//	15724	83709	87712	88620
497	81924	66606	00718	855//	16721	88620		
502	71928	62612	87912	6527/	12741	84705	85642	86359
628	52415	80018	96915	52400	11506	81710	85815	
715	42222	70016	95615	48400	11613	84815		
703	72644	64036	92115	754//	11729	87615		
827	52328	65016	99215	55400	11502	81710	85645	
817	62522	65026	96614	65500	11613	86621		
* 804	32631	65258	98314	38400	12307	83817		
809	52522	58216	98214	55300	11501	82707	85620	
894	72413	66216	02916	753//	15509	81708	83618	87640

only changed 0.7 mb. For a full explanation of all the figures in the code, reference should be made to the Daily Weather Report obtainable from the Meteorological Office.

Once station plots have been completed the isobars and fronts can be drawn in. The interpolation of isobars has already been described on page 30, while the location of any fronts can be done by identifying zones of rapid temperature change and in some cases sudden changes in the trend of isobars which indicate changes in wind direction.

Common weather patterns

The main weather systems have already been described in chapter 7 and need only be referred to briefly here. A typical depression is shown on the chart for 06 hours on 14 August 1979, figure 10.6. It shows a closed series of isobars with the lowest pressure at the centre, accompanied by a frontal system which in this case is rather complicated. A 'deep' depression is one in which the difference in pressure between the centre and the margins is rather large. In this case the difference is between 16 mb and 28 mb but the pressure change occurs in a fairly short distance, resulting in a steep pressure gradient and strong winds. Conversely a shallow depression has a small pressure difference between its centre and the margins and exhibits less severe pressure gradients.

A secondary depression is much smaller but it is often quite deep and frequently grows to replace the primary one as it, in its turn, declines. They frequently form on a trailing cold front and then proceed to circulate the main depression in an anticlockwise direction in the northern hemisphere. Such a secondary depression is shown over the Adriatic on the chart for 5 January 1979, figure 10.3.

An anticyclone is also depicted by a series of closed isobars but this time the pressure at the centre is higher than around the outside. Two anticyclones are shown on the chart for 00 hours on 5 January 1979, one located in the Atlantic, west of Ireland, and the other over Scandinavia. In general the isobars are more widely spaced in anticyclones and so winds are less strong. Also, because winds flow from high pressure towards low pressure and are deflected to the right in the northern hemisphere the circulation is clockwise, not anticlockwise as in a depression.

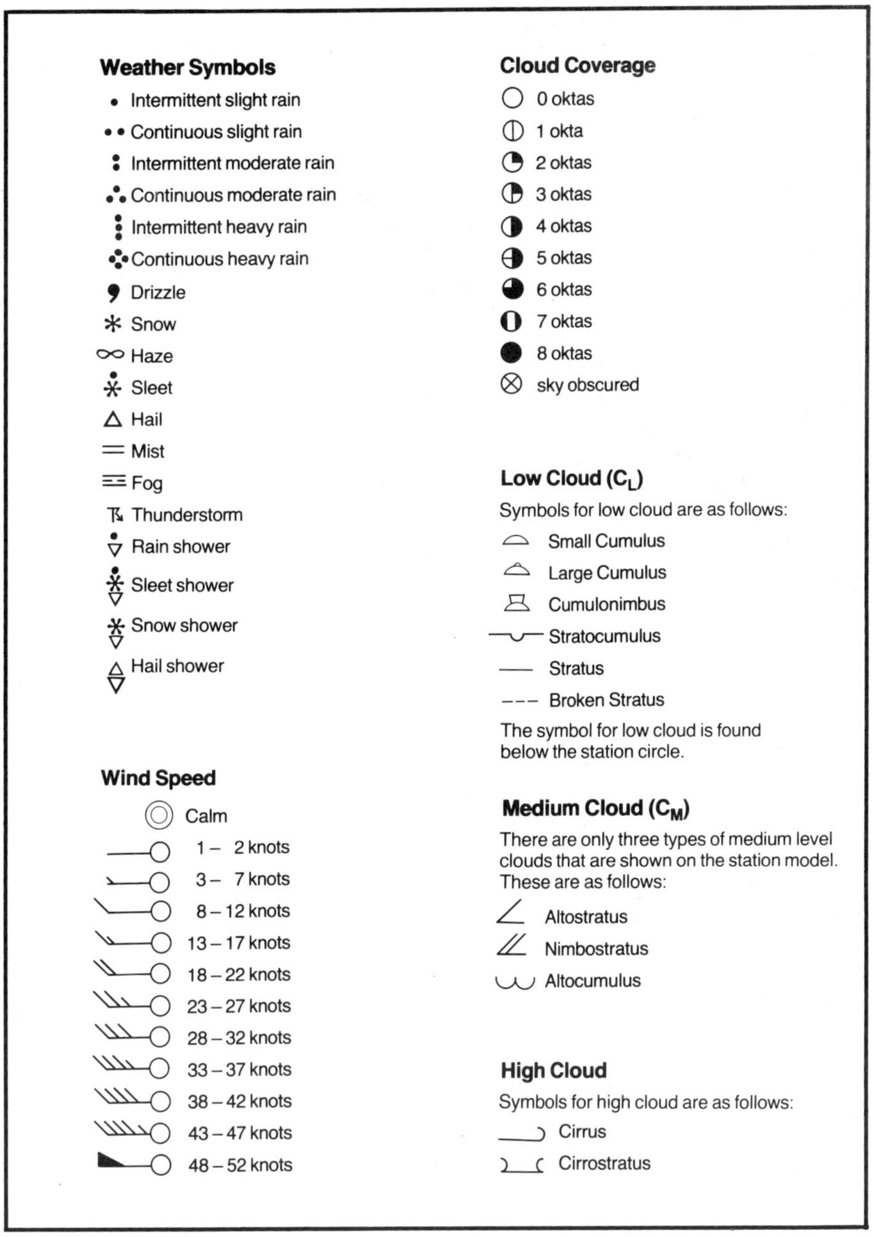

Weather Symbols
Intermittent slight rain
Continuous slight rain
Intermittent moderate rain
Continuous moderate rain
Intermittent heavy rain
Continuous heavy rain
Drizzle
Snow
Haze
Sleet
Hail
Mist
Fog
Thunderstorm
Rain shower
Sleet shower
Snow shower
Hail shower
Wind Speed
Calm
1 – 2 knots
3 – 7 knots
8 – 12 knots
13 – 17 knots
18 – 22 knots
23 – 27 knots
28 – 32 knots
33 – 37 knots
38 – 42 knots
43 – 47 knots
48 – 52 knots
Cloud Coverage
0 oktas
1 okta
2 oktas
3 oktas
4 oktas
5 oktas
6 oktas
7 oktas
8 oktas
sky obscured
Low Cloud (C_L)
Symbols for low cloud are as follows:
Small Cumulus
Large Cumulus
Cumulonimbus
Stratocumulus
Stratus
Broken Stratus
The symbol for low cloud is found below the station circle.
Medium Cloud (C_M)
There are only three types of medium level clouds that are shown on the station model. These are as follows:
Altostratus
Nimbostratus
Altocumulus
High Cloud
Symbols for high cloud are as follows:
Cirrus
Cirrostratus

Fig 10.2 The weather symbols

A ridge of high pressure is very similar to a spur on a contour map and appears as an extension of high pressure between two areas of low pressure. Such an area is to be seen over central Europe on the map in figure 10.3. The weather associated with a ridge is similar to that of an anticyclone but it is usually of shorter duration.

Troughs are shown by a similar V-shaped pattern of isobars, but this time pressure is low in the middle and the feature is similar to a valley on a contour map. Such a trough is visible to the west of Norway in figure 10.3.

A region between two centres of high pressure and two centres of low pressure is known as a col and such an area is shown over the British Isles on the chart for Thursday 13 July at 00 hours, figure 10.5. As in this case, a col often shows a marked absence of pressure change indicated by the lack of isobars, and so winds are light and variable. However, it is difficult to generalise about the weather associated with a col as much depends on the nature of the air mass and its immediate past history and on the adjacent pressure systems and the way they develop.

As in the case of a col, Britain is not always under the influence of a recognisable weather system and may find itself in the no man's land between systems. In this case it is easier to look at the kind of air stream that is affecting the country and the weather that is associated with it.

A northerly air flow is illustrated by the situation in the Baltic and over central Europe on the chart for 5 January 1979, figure 10.3. It results from the flow of air between a high pressure system over the Scandinavian Peninsula and a low to the east over Russia. If this occurs over Britain it brings cold air from the arctic southwards. During its journey over the Norwegian Sea it is warmed from below and so becomes highly unstable. The

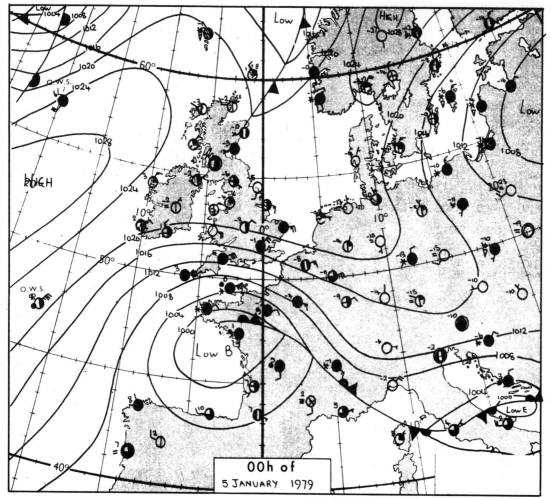

Fig 10.3 Weather chart for 00 hours Friday 5 January 1979

characteristic weather is therefore showers and bright intervals, while in winter heavy snowfall is likely especially over the mountains and north-facing slopes. Such weather is especially dangerous in spring when a northerly air flow can lead to frost which is damaging to young fruit blossom.

An easterly or northeasterly flow is shown over southern England on the same chart. This is caused by a low over western France and a ridge over the north of England and the North Sea. The source of air, as in this case, is frequently from Scandinavia or western Russia and in winter or spring will bring spells of intensely cold weather. In summer the weather is often fine with long, sunny spells and warm temperatures, but east coasts may be cloudy and heating during the day may trigger thunderstorms inland.

A southerly flow of air occurs over Britain when there is low pressure to the west and high pressure to the east. The chart for 06 hours on 14 August 1979 shows this set up over West Germany and Scandinavia, but it is not too common over Britain and is usually met in the autumn when there is high pressure over the continent and a depression approaches from the west. Such a situation is responsible for an 'Indian Summer' when unusually warm

and sunny weather is prevalent. However, the light flows of warm air can cause coastal fog and radiation fog may occur inland at night.

A southwesterly pattern of air flow is very common in Britain and occurs whenever depressions run northeastwards off the west coasts of Scotland and Norway. The nearest approach to such conditions is shown in the southern Irish Sea and in the western approaches to the English Channel on the chart for 06 hours on 14 August 1979, figure 10.6, but they are frequently associated with the passage of the warm sector of a depression. During such times mild, moist air spreads over the country giving poor visibility and much coastal fog. The sky is commonly overcast with stratus cloud very prominent and there may be prolonged drizzle.

A northwesterly flow of air usually follows the passage of a depression when pressure is low to the northeast over the North Sea and southern Scandinavia. This brings in clear polar air and results in excellent visibility. However, as the air crosses the Atlantic it picks up moisture and is heated from below becoming highly unstable. Sharp showers are therefore common and rain is especially heavy over high ground and western coasts.

Weather map analysis

The weather map presents a composite picture of a large amount of weather data and so in attempting to analyse the map it is helpful to take one aspect at a time. The same approach may also be used in tackling examination questions although, because of the time factor, it is likely that only some aspects of the weather situation will be covered.

(a) Pressure and winds

It is usually a good idea to begin by locating the main pressure systems on the chart. This can be done either by giving the position of the centre of each system or by drawing an analytical sketch map to show the pressure systems and their related fronts (see figure 10.4). In each case the value of the central pressure should be stated so revealing the range of pressure over the chart.

Wind direction is of course related to the pattern of isobars and near the ground winds will normally cross the isobars from high to low pressure at an oblique angle. This can be explained by reference to the coriolis force and the deflection of winds to the right of the northern hemisphere. Any anomalous wind directions will almost certainly be the result of local effects such as valley winds in areas of high

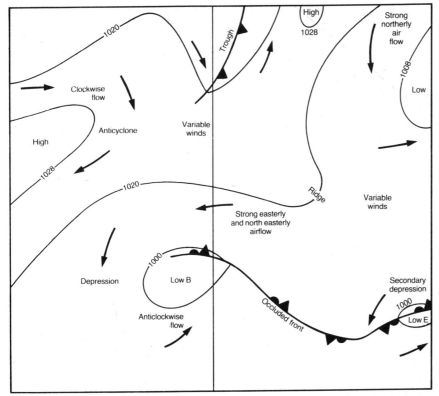

Fig 10.4 *Analytical map to show the distribution of pressure and winds for 00 hours Friday 5 January 1979*

(b) *Temperatures*

The temperature distribution over the chart is vital to any analysis of the weather. It is a good plan to quote the highest and lowest temperatures as well as the most common temperatures in different parts of the chart. Again anomalous temperatures will be the result of local conditions such as altitude or temperature inversions such as those that occur in valleys at night.

In accounting for the temperature it is most important to take note of the season of the year and the time of day. Temperature loss at night or gain by day also depends on cloud cover and the amount of wind, while the position of the fronts associated with any depression will indicate the location of air masses possessing noticeable temperature differences. Finally distance from the coast may also be a factor.

(c) *Cloud type and amount*

Cloud type is not normally given in examination questions, but both cloud amount and type are strongly influenced

relief or land and sea breezes along coasts. Wind speed depends on the pressure gradient so it is also important to refer to the spacing of the isobars in different parts of the chart.

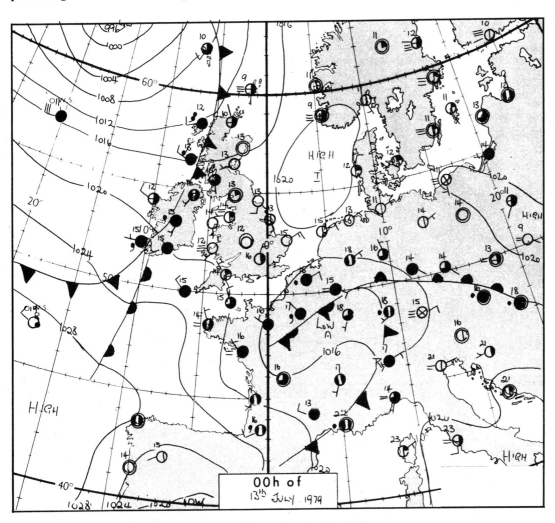

Fig 10.5 *Weather map for 00 hours on Thursday 13 July 1979*

by air masses and the way the air masses are being modifed, and by the development of frontal conditions. For example, polar air approaching the British Isles over the warm North Atlantic Drift is likely to be highly unstable and to possess large banks of cumulus cloud. The season of the year is also a factor and anticyclones are more likely to develop fog or stratus cloud in winter and cumulus cloud as a result of convective activity in summer. Other influences include altitude and relief, distance from the sea and wind direction.

(d) Weather conditions
The location of any precipitation and its type should be considered and can be related to cloud development associated with air masses and frontal systems. The type of precipitation is very dependent on the time of year, but the type of air mass and any convective activity are also important factors while others include altitude, wind direction and distance from the sea.

Other features of the weather such as mist or fog may in some cases be coastal, while in winter anticyclones are more likely to occur inland. Cloud cover, wind, altitude and relief all contribute to the formation of different types of fog.

Analysis of sample maps
Two maps have been chosen for analysis, one showing a depression to the south of Britain and the other a depression centred over the Irish Sea. In the first case an attempt will be made to analyse the whole map, while in the second a number of more specific questions will be answered.

Chart for 00 hours on 5 January 1979, figure 10.3.

(a) Pressure and winds
Pressure is high over Scandinavia and to the west of Ireland and in each case exceeds 1028 mb. A ridge of high pressure extends eastwards across the North Sea into central Europe giving a light northerly air flow of 3–7 knots over southern Sweden and East Germany, but low pressure over Russia is causing a stronger northerly flow of 13–17 knots over Finland and the Baltic Sea. In the absence of isobars over the North Sea, winds are extremely light to the east of Britain, and along the east coast and in central and eastern Europe wind direction is rather variable and more dependent on local conditions.

To the south of Britain a deep depression is centred over the Bay of Biscay with a central pressure of less than 1000 mb. As a result isobars are packed closely together, especially along the northern edge of the depression, giving a steep pressure gradient over southern Britain and the English Channel. The result is a strong easterly flow of 23–27 knots due to the anticlockwise circulation of air about the low pressure centre. An occluded front runs southeastwards across France and the depression is almost stationary and beginning to fill. A secondary depression can also be seen over the Adriatic.

(b) Temperatures
The range of temperature shown on the chart is from −27°C over Scandinavia to 10°C in north Spain, while in Britain it runs from −6°C to 3°C. The low temperature over central Sweden is partly due to the high latitude in winter, but also to the clear skies associated with the anticyclone. This is allowing for the loss of heat upwards by radiation during the night. For similar reasons air temperatures are low everywhere over the continental interior and so resulting in temperatures below freezing in southern England due to the easterly air flow. Further north in Britain where winds are less strong and the direction more variable, low temperatures are being experienced as a result of radiation losses at night. Only along the west coast where the effect of the Atlantic Ocean is most strongly felt are temperatures above freezing point. Elsewhere in Europe the occluded front is a zone of rapid temperature change. To the north they are universally below freezing and becoming more so with distance from the front, while to the south in Spain and France they are all above freezing and especially along the coast.

(c) Cloud cover
Cloud cover is generally light especially in areas of high pressure where air is subsiding and being warmed adiabatically. Typical of this situation are the northern half of Britain and central Europe. Rather higher cloud amounts are being recorded over the Baltic Sea and in southwest Norway, perhaps due to the presence of water surfaces, but there are clearly cloud patches over the whole area of the chart.

More consistent cloud cover is to be found along the front in France and northern Italy where air is being lifted up the frontal surface to give more continuous banks of cloud. Also associated with the depression is the belt of cloud cover over southern Britain and the English Channel which forms the largest area of cloud on the chart.

(d) Weather
The chart shows that a number of stations are experiencing mist or fog patches. Some in central Europe are clearly patches of radiation fog and in central Ireland and southern France it is almost certainly due to the same cause. Mist occurring on the North Sea coast of West Germany and the coast of Portugal may, however, be sea fog drifting in over the land.

Two areas of the chart are receiving significant snowfall. Air circling the low pressure over Russia is bringing snow to the coastal areas around the Baltic Sea and to parts of central Europe that lie in its path. Further snowfall is occurring along the occluded front in southeast France and over the English Channel.

Snowfall over southern Britain was in fact more significant than the chart suggests. Although falls were not heavy, and generally not more than 10–15 cm, there was considerable drifting in the strong to gale force easterly winds as might have been expected and there was considerable disruption of communications throughout southwest England.

Sample questions and answers
Chart for 06 hours Tuesday 14 August 1979, figure 10.6.

1 Construct the weather report that might be received by the meteorological office from a ship located in the North Sea at 57°N 2°E.

Wind: 160°, 14 knots; temperature: 16°C; pressure: 994.6 mb; pressure tendency: fall of 3.4 mb; 6 oktas of sky covered; type of cloud: strato-cumulus, cumulus and cumulo-nimbus.

2 Describe and account for the direction and strength of the winds over the British Isles. Why are the winds lighter and more variable over Spain?

The winds are blowing in an anticlockwise direction around a centre near Dublin giving northeasterly winds in northern Scotland, northerly winds in western Ireland, northwesterlies over southwest Ireland, westerlies over the Scillies, southwest to south winds over southern Britain and southeasterlies in northern England and southeast Scotland. This pattern is a result of the fact that winds blow from high pressure

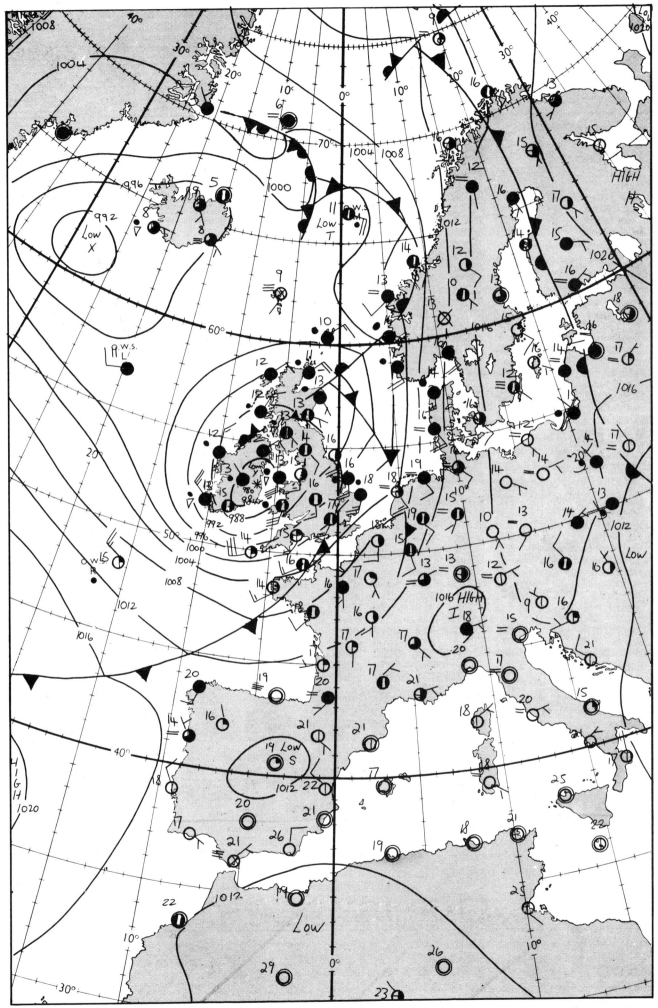

Fig 10.6   Weather map for 06 hours Tuesday 14 August 1979

to low pressure but are deflected to the right in the northern hemisphere by the coriolis force. The winds are strong, varying from 3–7 knots in eastern Scotland to 28-32 knots over southwest England and the Irish Sea. This is typical of a deep depression where winds tend to be supergeostrophic and where the isobars are closely spaced giving a steep pressure gradient.

The winds are lighter over Spain due to the small pressure gradient indicated by the relative absence of isobars. The circulation has a tendency to be anticlockwise about a low pressure area in the centre of Spain but there are a number of anomalous wind directions. These include Gibraltar and Faro in southern Portugal which appear to show a clockwise circulation, and Valencia where the wind seems to be blowing at right angles to the isobars. In the absence of a strong pressure gradient the pattern of isobars exerts only a weak control over wind direction and local influences such as land and sea breezes or valley winds are more prominent. Some winds are more influenced by neighbouring pressure systems than by that over central Spain.

3 Referring to the nature of a depression, try to explain why:
(i) It is raining on the coast of East Anglia.
(ii) Rain showers are occurring in southwest Ireland.
(iii) Sleet and snow are falling near Dublin although it is summer.

(i) The coast of East Anglia is close to an approaching cold front where warm air is being lifted over a wedge of cold air. The resulting expansion of the rising air mass causes consistent adiabatic cooling and condensation resulting in steady rainfall.
(ii) Southwest Ireland lies in a stream of cool polar air which has been flowing over the warm surface of the North Atlantic. The result has been considerable warming from below and the addition of moisture making the air mass highly unstable. Strong convective activity has caused cloud to bubble up producing sharp but rather localised rain showers.
(iii) Dublin lies in the same air stream as southwest Ireland and is experiencing somewhat similar conditions. Temperatures over the map suggest that the land is warmer than the sea and that in general, temperatures rise towards the east. This would increase convective activity and increase the vertical development of the cloud. At high levels in the cloud it will be cold enough for snow to form although hail is more typical of this situation. As they fall the snowflakes tend to melt but in this case they are reaching the ground only partially melted to give sleet.

4 Discuss the temperature in Gorleston (53°N 1°E) compared with that at Scilly (50°N 6°W) and Lerwick (60°N 1°W) giving reasons for the differences observed.

Gorleston has a temperature of 18°C and has the highest temperature of the three stations quoted. Although it lies between two cold fronts it is generally in the warm sector of the depression and is therefore being affected by a warm tropical maritime air mass.

In contrast the Isles of Scilly with 14°C are behind the cold front in a polar maritime air mass while Lerwick at 10°C occupies a similar position in front of the warm front. The difference in temperature between Lerwick and Scilly may result from the difference in latitude, but it is more likely that the polar air affecting Scilly has been warmed by its long sea track over the North Atlantic Drift.

5 Assuming that by 18 hours on 14 August the depression will be centred over the North Sea, describe the changes in the weather you would expect for Gorleston over the next 12 hours.

For an hour or so the wind will remain strong and southerly with a wind speed of 23–27 knots and the sky will be overcast. It will continue to rain and the temperature will remain at 18°C or fall slightly.

With the passage of the second cold front there will be a significant drop in temperature to 16°C and a further drop in temperature is likely, to perhaps as low as 12°C. The wind will veer to southwest and then west and strengthen to 28–37 knots.

The sky will partially clear to give clear intervals and a cloud cover of 3–7 oktas. The continuous rain will cease and be replaced by occasional heavy showers.

Throughout the 12 hour period the pressure will continue to fall reaching 988 mb or below, but it will stabilize during the last three hours and perhaps begin to rise again as the depression moves away northeastwards towards Scandinavia.

EXERCISES

With reference to the chart for 00 hours on 13 July 1979, figure 10.5:
10.1 Describe the pattern of air flow over the British Isles. Why are the winds generally light in character?
10.2 Can you recognise any pattern in the distribution of temperature over the British Isles? What factors do you think might have influenced this pattern?
10.3 It could be said that the chart indicates an absence of weather over the British Isles. Explain what you think such a statement implies.
10.4 Attempt to give a forecast for the London area over the next 24 hours. Try to explain any difficulties you face in giving such a forecast.

Booklist

B W Atkinson, *The Weather Business*, Aldus, 1968

R G Barry, and R J Chorley, *Atmosphere, Weather and Climate*, Methuen, 1971

R G Barry, and A H Perry, *Synoptic Climatology*, Methuen, 1973

M Bradshaw, *Earth, the Living Planet*, Hodder & Stoughton, 1977

D Bowen, *Britain's Weather*, David and Charles, 1969

T J Chandler, *Modern Meteorology and Climatology*, Nelson, 1972

R Geiger, *The Climate Near the Ground*, Harvard University Press, 1965

J Hanwell, *Atmospheric Processes*, George Allen & Unwin, 1980

W J Maunder, *The Value of the Weather*, Methuen, 1970

D E Pedgley, *A Course in Elementary Meteorology*, H.M.S.O., 1962

A H Perry, *Environmental Hazards in the British Isles*, George Allen & Unwin, 1981

A H Perry and V C Perry, *Weather Maps*, Oliver & Boyd, 1975

A H Perry and J M Walker, *The Ocean-Atmosphere System*, Longman, 1977

R K Pilsbury, *Clouds and Weather*, Batsford, 1969

H Riehl, *Introduction to the Atmosphere*, McGraw-Hill, 1965

D Riley and L Spolton, *World Weather and Climate*, Cambridge University Press, 1974

R C Sutcliffe, *Weather and Climate*, Weidenfeld and Nicolson, 1966

O G Sutton, *Understanding the Weather*, Pelican, 1960

C E Wallington, *Your own Weather Map*, Royal Meteorological Society, 1967

P G Wickham, *The Practice of Weather Forecasting*, H.M.S.O. 1970

Acknowledgements

Photographs: John Cleare fig 8.6; Bruce Coleman, fig 5.9a; R.K. Pilsbury figs 5.9b, c, d, e, 5.18a, b, c, d, e, f, g, h, j, k; Thomson Holidays fig 8.7; John Topham fig 2.3a, b, d, 8.3; Western Times fig 2.3c.

Drawings adapted or reproduced from: *Atmospheric Processes* by Hanwell, published by George Allen and Unwin figs 5.15, 6.4, 6.9, 8.8; Crown Copyright, reproduced with permission of the Controller of Her Majesty's Stationery Office figs 10.3, 5 and 6; *Earth, the Living Planet* by Bradshaw, Abbot and Gelsthorpe, published by Hodder and Stoughton fig 8.9; *Modern Meteorology and Climatology* by Chandler, published by Thomas Nelson fig 6.16; *Skin of the Earth* by Miller, published by Associated Book Publishers Ltd fig 5.12; *World Weather and Climate* by Riley and Spolton, published by Cambridge University Press figs 2.1, 6.13.

Index